Cultural China

A Reader 中國讀本 on China

Su Shuyang

Better Link Press

This book is edited and designed by the Editorial Committee of *Cultural China* series.

Managing Directors: Wang Youbu, Xu Naiqing
Editorial Director: Wu Ying
Editors: Wu Ying, Patrick Wallace

Translation by Chen Zijian
Interior and Cover Design: Yuan Yinchang, Li Jing

ISBN 978-1-60220-103-3

Address any comments about *A Reader on China* to:

Better Link Press
99 Park Ave
New York, NY 10016
USA
or
Shanghai Press and Publishing Development Company
F7, Donghu Road, Shanghai, China (200031)
Email: comments_betterlinkpress@hotmail.com

Computer typeset by Yuan Yinchang Design Studio, Shanghai
Printed in China by Shanghai Donnelley Printing Co. Ltd.

1   2   3   4   5   6   7   8   9   10

CONTENTS

CONTENTS

Prologue

More than 2000 years ago in early summer (278 BC), on the fifth of May in the Chinese lunar calendar, a gaunt, pallid gray-haired old man ran up and down the banks of Miluo River in anguished torment. The wind blew, the clouds danced and the river flowed. The man mumbled to himself and screamed towards heaven. Then, he clasped a heavy stone to his chest and cast himself into the river. An official of the Chu kingdom, he was the great poet Qu Yuan.

Grieving people from all around rushed to the scene, rowing out in small boats to try to find his body, throwing bamboo tubes filled with glutinous rice into the water to feed his spirit. Every year since then on that day, people honor the memory of this man who cared deeply for his nation and its people by racing boats and making *zongzi* (pyramid-shaped dumplings of glutinous rice wrapped in bamboo or reed leaves). The ritual has been observed for more than 2000 years.

What started out as an occasion to recover Qu Yuan's body and honor the dead soul eventually came to be known as the Dragon Boat Festival (5th of May in the Chinese lunar calendar), a traditional festival of the Chinese nation. The memory of this poet gradually faded into the folklore and legend, and has become institutionalized as a part of the Chinese culture, a rare occurrence in human history. His body was never found, left instead to rejoin the water and soil of his motherland.

Qu Yuan wrote in his great poem, *Li Sao*, that he hated both the mighty and corrupt, and the lowly and perfidious, wishing nothing else but to ride in a heavenly chariot with great and noble forebears. "When a little delightful glimpse is caught of one's hometown amid the golden glow of dawn, the driver cannot hide his sorrow, and the horse is overcome with emotion and will not walk another step." This feeling for the motherland is universal to the Chinese.

Let us now ride in that heavenly chariot and look at this land and its people.

Chapter One Land without End

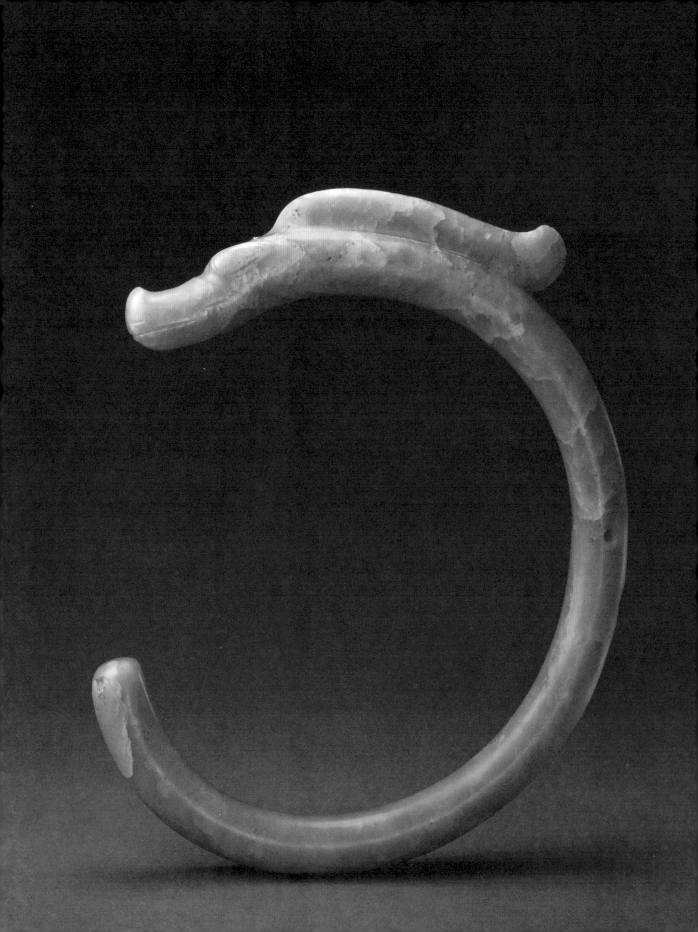

—

World Creating Mythology

Pan Gu Separates Heaven And Earth

What is the world? Why do the vast sky, the great wilderness, the raging rivers and the vast oceans exist? Why are there stars, moon, wind, rain, thunder and lightning? Why flowers, grasses, high mountains and low plains? These are ancient questions of humanity.

Even when humans were naught but barbarians, they had tried to answer these questions. They used what knowledge they had to expand their imaginations and explain the world around them, creating the earliest myths of creation. While some of these stories were later validated by archaeology, some were just wild imaginings of ancient peoples.

Every culture has its own creation myth. The Chinese myth of "Pan Gu" is unique and vivid.

Legend has it that in the beginning, all was blackness and emptiness. Then, suddenly, a small bubble appeared. The bubble became a ball of smoke, which

Left: A jade dragon

11

Pan Gu, who separated heaven and earth

then began to coalesce. It grew and grew for a millennia, eventually becoming a red, egg-shaped object.

This was the gestating Pan Gu. After 18,000 years, he awoke. Appalled by the infinite blackness, he threw open his arms and legs to break the suffocating emptiness, separating heaven and earth. If this truly happened, how clear must that first beam of sacred light have been passing down through the firmament. The clear and light positive energies (*yang*) rose gradually, becoming the sky. The turbid and heavy negative energies (*yin*) descended gradually, becoming the earth. The shards of Pan Gu's shell either rose to the heavens and become stars or fell to earth and became minerals. But the breach between heaven and earth was not large enough; Pan Gu was still confined. He would not let the opening close up again, returning to void. So he planted his feet firmly on the ground, put his hands on the sky and forced it further apart. From then on, the sky became one *zhang* (3.3m) higher, the earth one *zhang* thicker, and Pan Gu one *zhang* taller every day. After 18,000 years, Pan Gu had grown to a height of 90,000 *li* (or 45,000 km), his head in the sky and feet on the ground, defining the distance as *jiu chong tian*, or "nine heavens".

The realm of Pan Gu was of high intelligence. The sky was clear when he was pleased, and darkened when he was angry. The wind blew when he sighed, and his tears became rain. Lightning streaked across the sky when he blinked and thundered when he snored.

Pan Gu lived untold lonely years in this domain of his making, and then finally perished. This body which separated the sky and earth fell to the ground with a crash. His left eye became the sun and the right the moon. His head

became Mount Tai in the east. His upturned feet became
Mount Hua in the west. His belly became Mount Song in the
middle. His left arm became Mount Heng in the south and his
right Mount Heng in the north. His arteries now are our rivers, his

An ancient
bone implement

veins, mountain ridges and roads. His flesh is our rich, fertile soil. His hairs are the
plants. His teeth and bones became gold and jade. His sweat is now our dew,
providing moisture to the life on earth.

The great ancestor used to hold up the sky above. The land we walk upon
used to be his flesh and blood. This myth binds all Chinese to their motherland
in heart, mind and spirit, and is an attachment which will never fade.

The myth of Pan Gu is not only popular among the Han people, but among
all the peoples of China, for while the names of the characters may change, the
myth is common to all. In every story, the hero separates heaven and earth
through his own labor. The theme of the great ancestor opening up the world
through hard work is universal to the Chinese. Born of land and sky, and having
begun the world by his own toil, this god is the unique spiritual embodiment of
the Chinese.

Nü Wa Patches Up The Sky

The world opened up by Pan Gu is said to be round in heaven and square on
earth. The heaven is held up by four great columns, and the earth secured with
rope. As time went by, the columns began to rot and the land began to crack.
Lava and putrid water oozed up from underground. The sky dropped rain, hail,
and meteors day and night.

Fuxi and Nü Wa

One year, the gods of fire and water, Zhu Rong and Gong Gong fought each other. Gong Gong was defeated and fled to the ends of the sky. Zhu Rong gave chase and Gong Gong was cornered and pushed into Buzhou Mountain, one of the main columns of the sky. It cracked, and "the sky tilted to the northwest and the land sank to the southeast." A gaping hole appeared in the northwestern sky, and the celestial river fell through it and onto the land below as a massive earthquake began; flood and fires wreaked havoc. This roused the great black dragon who lived in the Central Plains and he, too, began to destroy. Suddenly all was blackness, fire and death.

Dancing and singing figures on a cliff

The catastrophe spread all over the universe, becoming the scourge of humanity. The heavenly mother of mankind, Nü Wa, could not bear to see her children suffer so. So she traveled to every corner of the world to find stones of five colors — red, yellow, blue, white and black — and piles of firewood to smelt them. The fire burned seven days and seven nights, melting the stones. She used the liquid to patch the sky. Then she went to the Great Sea and found a turtle. She removed its four legs and used them to replace the pillars of the sky. She slew the terrible dragon and banished the wild animals to the forests. She took the ash from smelting the stones and spread it over the flooded fields, making them flat again. The land and sky largely returned to normal, with only the sky in the northwest and the land in the southeast remaining unmendable and a little more tilted than before. So now, the sun and stars fall into the west and the rivers all flow to the southeast.

The Vast Territory

Pan Gu opened up our realm, and it is formed of his flesh and blood. The burly Gong Gong repaired the land, and Nü Wa the sky.

If we could fly over the lands in a heavenly chariot, we would see that the country is a place of huge steps, rising from the east to the west, little by little, until by the utmost west, and you would feel that you could almost step off the land into the celestial kingdom.

This heavenly stairway faces the Pacific Ocean with its back to the rest of Asia. Situated in eastern and middle part of Asia, it commands huge amounts of land and waters, a vast territory, a beautiful landscape and bountiful resources. Covering an area of approximately 9.6 million square kilometers, it is almost as large as all of Europe, and one of the largest countries in the world.

The country is 5,200 kilometers east to west and 5,500 kilometers north to south. The uttermost north, the center of the Heilongjiang River in northern Mohe, Heilongjiang Province and the uttermost south, Zengmu Shoal of Nansha Islands, are separated by nearly 50 degrees of latitude. When there is a blizzard in the north, the flowers are still bright in the south. The farthest point east,

The Pamirs

the convergence of the Heilongjiang and Wusuli Rivers, and the western edge on the Pamirs are 60 degrees of latitude apart. When the sun is rising in the east, the west remains bathed in moonlight.

Three Tiers of the Territory

The territory, composed of three tiers increasing in its elevation from the east to the west, is wonderfully varied, as towering mountains, cold, forbidding plateaus, shimmering lakes, rolling hills and boundless plains blend with each other.

Mount
Qomolangma

The First Tier

The Qinghai-Tibet Plateau, known as the "Roof of the World" is the highest in the world, its average height being 4 kilometers above sea level. The Himalayas and Mount Qomolangma (Everest) stand, spirit-like, at the juncture of the Chinese and Nepalese borders. At 8848.13 meters above sea level, it is both the highest and youngest place on earth, having only risen from the sea 30 million years ago.

Snow caps all the mountains and ridges on the plateau. When it melts, it surges down in raging rivers. Many of the great rivers of Asia, such as the Yangtze, Yellow and Yarlung Zhangbo Rivers, start here, making it the source of a truly impressive amount of hydropower. It is a marvelous plateau, whose rough exterior conceals a vivacious interior truly worthy of admiration and inspiring awe.

No other plateau in the world numbers its lakes anywhere near the 1,000-odd lakes of the Qinghai-Tibet Plateau, among them Nam Co, the highest lake in the world and Qinghai, the largest saltwater lake in the country. The mirror-like inland lakes scattered throughout the Plateau are truly exciting sights.

The country also contains numberless basins, home to lakes and flowers, dotting the landscape like pearls. The Qaidam Basin, the largest inland basin in the world, is found here along with 24 salt lakes that hold an estimated 60 billion tons of salt, accounting for almost half the total salt in the country.

At the north of the Qinghai-Tibet Plateau are the Kunlun and Qilian Mountains. To the east are the Hengduan Mountains. From here to the southeast and northwest, the terrain drops to the level of the second tier.

A musical instrument from Xinjiang

The Second Tier

The vast area from the Kunlun, Qilian and Hengduan Mountains to Greater Xing'an, Taihang, Wu and Xuefeng Mountains forms a lower tier 1 to 2 thousand meters above sea level.

Here, there are three large plateaus and basins.

The Inner Mongolian, Loess and Yunnan-Guizhou Plateaus, in that order from north to south, are the major plateaus of this tier.

The Inner Mongolia Plateau is approximately 1,000 meters above sea level and the second largest plateau in the country, with wide-open plains and plentiful grassland and water. It is the birthplace of the northern peoples of the nation. The Zhahai ancient relic of the Red Mountain Culture, found in the Mongolian Autonomous County of Fuxing, Liaoning Province, has pushed back the beginnings of Chinese cultural history about 3,000 years. There has been nearly 8,000 years of history from the time of the Red Mountain Culture until now. The Red Mountain dragon, an iconic element of their culture, is indicative of the intelligence of the ancients. The heroic ancestors of the nation prospered on the grassy plateau and left their mark on the Chinese history. They, along with the Huaxia peoples of the Central Plains, made important contributions to shaping history.

The Loess Plateau ranges from 800 to 2,000 meters above sea level and is covered with between 50 and 80 meters of silt. Much of the Chinese nation came into being on this very plateau, making it the birthplace of one of four major civilizations of the world. Proceeding east from the plateau along the Yellow River Valley, what unfolds before you is something of a walking tour through Chinese history. Zhou, Qin, Han, and Tang Dynasties silently tell their stories to you through the relics of their times.

The Yunnan-Guizhou Plateau is in the southwest of the country, filled with typical limestone (karst) topography. Mysterious stone forests, precipitous stone peaks, hidden caves, subterranean rivers, sometimes visible and sometimes invisible, all make up a dynamic terrain. Such a large area of karst topography is quite rare. The Huangguoshu Falls, situated in the upper reaches of the Dabang tributary of the Beipan River, drops 74 meters into Rhino Pond. The sheer sound and energy of these falls, largest in the country, make your spirit soar. This Plateau is the birthplace of the southwestern Chinese nationalities. Fossils of ancient apes, ancient great apes, hominids and Homo sapiens found here reveal that it is also a birthplace of humans. The ancestors of the Chinese nation were probably born here, a home common to modern Chinese.

The Qinghai-Tibet, of the first tier, and the Inner Mongolian, Loess and Yunnan-Guizhou Plateaus of the second tier are the four largest plateaus of China. There are three large basins on the second tier, namely, the Junggar, Tarim and Sichuan.

The Junggar Basin connects China to Central Asia. Lying in the extreme northwest of China in the Xinjiang Uygur Autonomous Region, nestled among the Tian and Altai Mountains, it looks like a great heavenly triangular pancake. It is 1,120 kilometers across and 800 kilometers from north to south at its widest, with an area of 380,000 square meters. It has an average altitude of 500-1,000

A musical instrument from Xinjiang

The Huangguoshu
Falls in Guizhou
Province

meters, though the surface of Aibi Lake is only 190 meters above sea level.
Though the Irtysh River flows northward to the Arctic, other nearby rivers like
the Manas and Wulungu flow into the Basin, forming lakes. Along the edge of
the Basin are beautiful hills and oases, now home to ranches with thousands
upon thousands of frolicking sheep. Vast expanses of wheat and cotton fields
paint the hills verdant green, pure white and shimmering gold. The floodplain
at the north of the basin has recently become farmlands where row after row
of great poplars grow, defending the boundless fields. Underground lay ample
deposits of oil and coal to power the great industrious nation.

The Tarim Basin is the largest inland basin in the world. Its center is the
largest desert in China, the Taklamakan. This place has been known as the
"place forbidden to life", and within its bounds Lop Nor has been known as

the "sea of death." Here sand and wind are the only earthly company to the sun and moon. Interestingly, in the Mongolian language, Lop Nor means "lake that receives great waters." In ancient times, this place was the Puchanghai Sea. It is 3,006 square meters, and is 768 meters above sea level. The prosperous Lolan Kingdom was founded in this place rich in water and grasses. The ancient Silk Road, connecting East to West, passed through here, and the ringing of camel bells played in the endless distance. Now, the sounds of bells ringing, horses neighing and instruments playing linger on only in the ruins of ancient kingdoms, as the sounds of rocket tests fill the sky. Modern-day explorers retrace the steps and honor the memories of their ancestors.

The Sichuan Basin is the "kingdom of heaven" of China. A warm, moist climate, fertile land and strong rivers give this place great resources, giving rise to a large population, and making it a paradise for any Chinese. It is the birthplace of the Bashu culture. The skill, intelligence, optimism, generosity and unfettered imagination of the ancients, evinced by the Sanxindui antiques recently excavated in Guanghan, will astonish you. Some scholars say that the Ciyoujiuli people, one of three ancestral peoples of China, used to be active in this area, explaining the great fertility of the land.

The round Turpan Depression, 245 kilometers across and 75 kilometers north to south can also be found in the Taklamakan Desert. Aiding Lake (Jueluohuan) at its center has the lowest elevation in China, its surface being 154 meters below sea level. The climate here is harsh, and the lake used to known as the lake of fire. In summer, it is the hottest place in the country. The Mountain of Flame is right here. Though the climate is hot and dry, through clever irrigation of karez (a system of underground channel-connected wells), the three local treasures, cotton, grapes and sweet melon grow well here. The troubles suffered here by Tang Monk and his companions in the "Journey to the West," though whimsical, are based on reality. How marvellous it would be to construct a giant fan in the sky and cool this place down, though keep it as productive as it is!

Beyond the Greater Xing'an, Taihang, Wu and Xuefeng Mountains lies the third tier of the territory.

The Third Tier

This third tier consists of those places with an altitude of less than 500 meters. The Northeast, North China and Yangtze River plains are, from north to south, the Great Plains of China.

A utensil from Xinjiang

The Northeast Plain is one of the "barns" of the country. People depend on the golden crops growing in its black soil, and its underground black gold. As the home to the Manchu and other peoples, it is an important part of Chinese culture and one of its birthplaces. The history of Lao Jin constitutes a glorious phase in the country's ancient history.

On the boundless North China Plain grow many varieties of fruits and corns. For aeons now, these plains have been the stage for many a tragic drama. The battle for the Central Plains has become synonymous with the idea of life-or-death struggle for controlling the whole country. Were it not for this plain, China would not exist as it does.

The Middle and Lower Yangtze Valley Plains are another birthplace of Chinese civilization. Like the Yellow River, the Yangtze is a mother river. The area has a good climate, dense population, numerous towns and good communication. From here China first had contact with the outside world early in its history. These plains now drive China'a modernization.

These three plains are nearly contiguous, like a great verdant seamless carpet of beauty and wealth having fallen from the sky.

On the edges of the plains lie gently rolling hills. To the south of the middle and lower reaches of the Yangtze River and the east of the Yunnan-Guizhou Plateau are Jiangnan Hills.

These plains continue to the sea, forming the continental shelf, which, along with the coastal islands, adorn the neck of the country just as a string of pearls.

Territorial Sea and Territorial Sky

China has vast maritime territory to match its vast land territory. On September 4th, 1958, China proclaimed that its territorial waters extend 12 nautical miles from its coast.

China's coastal area is in total approximately 4,730,000 square meters. The length of the continental coastline is 18,000-odd kilometers, containing over 5,000 islands of varying sizes, including the South China Sea Islands. The Bohai Sea, the Yellow Sea, the East China Sea and the South China Sea make up a vast nautical territory and are bounded by a long and meandering coastline. The numerous islands and the land area give China its immense size.

The eastward slant downward of Chinese lands is clearly the product of geology and not the bumping of Gong Gong's head again the Buzhou Mountain. Thus the tilted lands of the country face the sea in the east and are made warm and moist by the ocean air blowing inland. The surging east-bound rivers of the nation connect the southwest and the east, facilitating its communications and affording immense hydropower through the strength of falling waters through the many tiers of the land. And the broad seas give us salt, fish and whatever undiscovered riches may lurk on the ocean floor.

The Charms of the Territory

A Mountainous Country

Mountainous areas of the country comprise over two-thirds of the total land area. This means that arable land is limited.

The country's mountain ranges can be divided into three categories:

First, the mountains running east to west are divided into three sub-ranges: the northernmost is comprised of the Tianshan Mountains and the Yinshan Mountains; the middle section is the Kunlun and the Qinling Mountains; the southern tier is the Nanling Mountains.

Second, the mountains running northeast to southwest are also divided into three sub-ranges: the westernmost includes the Greater Xing'an Mountains, the Taihang Mountains, the Wushan Mountains and the Xuefeng Mountains; the middle is made up of Changbai Mountain and Wuyi Mountain. The easternmost section is the Taiwan Mountains.

Third, mountains running from the northwest to the southeast are the Altai Mountains and the Qilian Mountains

In addition, the Himalayas connect with the Hengduan Mountains, both forming a huge mountainous arc.

Rivers and Lakes

Spread over the country's vast territory are numerous large rivers that roll on incessantly. There are more than 1,500 of these rivers, draining a total area of over 1,000 square kilometers. The aggregate annual river runoff is 2.7 trillion cubic meters, ranking sixth in the world, while the volume of total water resources proudly ranks first. Total water reserves have the power generation potential of 680 million kilowatts; of this number, 370 million kilowatts can be readily produced.

The country's rivers flow mainly west to east directly into the sea; some pour into the Pacific Ocean, among them the Yangtze River, the Yellow River, the Heilongjiang River and the Zhujiang River. A few flow southward into the Indian Ocean, like the Yarlung Zangbo River and the Nujiang River.

Right: The Yarlung Zangbo River in Tibet

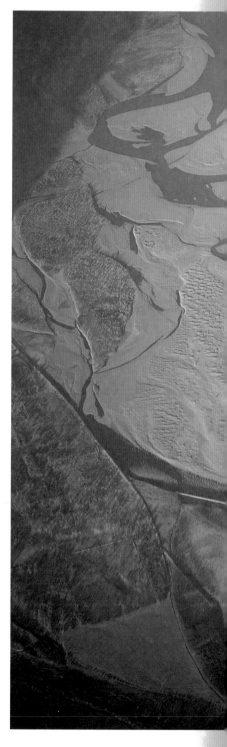

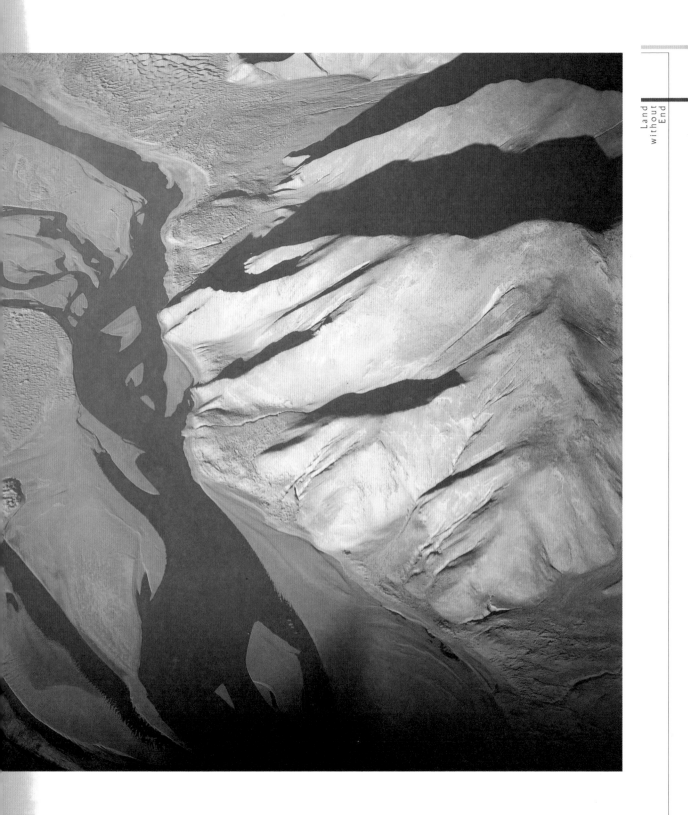

Only the lonely Irtysh River makes a path to the Arctic Ocean. The rivers that flow into the oceans are called outbound rivers; the others, called inland rivers, either disappear into the deserts or flow into inland lakes. The Tarim River in Xingjiang is the largest inland river in the country.

The surging Yangtze River is the largest river in the country. With a length of 6,300 kilometers, it ranks number three in the world. It originates in the western part of Qinghai Province, and its main stream winds through 11 provinces and autonomous regions before emptying into the East China Sea. The Yangtze River Basin accounts for approximately one-fifth of the total area of China. The Yangtze River greatly facilitates river traffic, in addition to its importance to irrigation. Its main stream and tributaries are a rich water resource, accounting for approximately 40% of the total for the whole country.

The Yellow River is China's mother river; China's ancient civilization was born on its banks. This river also originates in Qinghai Province, flows through nine provinces and autonomous regions, then pours into the Bohai Sea. Its total length is 5,464 kilometers. Over the centuries, the course of the Yellow River has changed several times. The surging yellow water has both contributed to the welfare of the people, and inflicted damage. The history of the Chinese nation parallels the struggle with the Yellow River.

Apart from natural rivers, the country also has many man-made rivers — canals. The Grand Canal, which was opened during the reign of Emperor Yang of the Sui Dynasty, at one time connected the south of China with the north. It goes directly from Hangzhou to Beijing. With a total length of 1,794 kilometers, it is the longest canal in the country - indeed, in the world. This main water artery connecting the south and the north is now being dredged; some day, it will be possible to embark on a boat in Beijing to travel all the way to the "Paradises" of Suzhou and Hangzhou.

The country also has numerous lakes draping the breast of the motherland like pearls - there are over 130 lakes larger than 100 square kilometers in area. In addition to natural lakes, China has many artificial lakes — reservoirs.

Along the middle and lower Yangtze Valley plains freshwater lakes abound. Among the lakes are the country's largest, Boyang Lake; the second largest, Dongting Lake, the third largest, Taihu Lake, and the smaller Hongze and Chaohu Lakes.

The Qinghai-Tibet Plateau contains more total volume of lake water than any other plateau in the world. Most of its lakes are inland salt lakes. Qinghai Lake is the largest of them. This lake abounds with gymnocypris przewalskii (a kind of carp), so countless flocks of birds nest on islands in the lake, chirping and flapping their white-feathered wings, as they happily and freely soar like angels in the vast sky and over the water. This is a paradise for birds.

The lakes on the Yunnan-Guizhou Plateau were mostly formed by the sinking of broken strata. Because of the water-filtering quality of limestone, lake water is limpid and beautiful. Dianchi Pond in the southern suburb of Kunming presents an attractive appearance and amiable atmosphere.

These numerous lakes provide the convenience of water transport for us. The water itself is a resource for consumption. All this is in addition to their contribution in terms of crop irrigation and electric power generation.

As the rivers and lakes nourish the country, they also bring disaster. From the legend "Da Yu Leading the People in Curbing Floods", we know how much the people's ancestors suffered. The descendants of Da Yu have inherited the resolve and capacity to fight floods. It is necessary to continue to learn, to strive to preserve both the water and the soil, and to dredge rivers in order be better prepared for the vagaries of nature.

The bird island on the Qinghai Lake

What is even more terrible than floods is drought, with thousands of square kilometers of parched lands on which every green thing wilts. In the ancient legend, "Yi Shooting Nine Suns", the description of "nine suns rising at the same time" is an apt portrayal of drought. While the banks of the Yangtze River overflow, and floods in the Yangtze River Valley surge, the Yellow River dries up day by day. Efforts must be redoubled to ensure that the waters of the Yellow River never dry up and keep flowing without stop, eternally providing nourishment.

Beautiful Coastline

Most of China's rivers flow eastward toward the sea. The country faces the Pacific, and is also embraced from north to south by the Bohai Sea, the Yellow Sea, the East China Sea and South China Sea. The country's coastline is long and sinuous: From the mouth of the Yalu River on the Yellow sea at China's border with North Korea, to the mouth of the Beilun River on the border with Vietnam in the south, the total length is 18,000 kilometers. Along this coastline are numerous harbors.

**A pretty
handicraft piece**

The coastal areas of the country can be divided into two main types: the region north of Hangzhou Bay has mainly sand coasts, which are flat, shallow and broad, while the region south of Hangzhou Bay is largely composed of rocky coasts. The latter have deep water and long coastlines, making most of them natural and high-quality harbors. This division of coastal types is only a rough one: rocky coasts are also found in the sand coast belt, as are sandy beaches in the south. The redwood-covered coasts of Fujian and Guangdong Provinces, the coral reef coasts of south Taiwan and the fault coast of east Taiwan make the country's coastlines even more colorful.

The country's harbors can also be divided into two kinds. The first are river-mouth harbors, spreading at places where large rivers enter the sea. Among them are Tianjin, Shanghai, and Guangzhou. The second kind are those formed geologically without rivers, such as Dalian, Qinhuangdao, Qingdao, Zhanjiang, Beihai, Haikou, Jilong and Gaoxiong.

It is not an exaggeration to depict the country as one with a huge number of islands. Offshore of the long coastline are over 5000 of them. The Zhoushan Archipelago and the South China Sea Islands are both masses of huge islands.

**A view of
Shanghai's Pudong**

The largest two islands are Taiwan and Hainan. The total island area is over 80,000 square kilometers.

The Broad Sea

The country faces a broad expanse of sea. At one time in history, China was the strongest seafaring country, having the world's largest fleet. Its mariners never killed nor plundered; instead, they conducted civilized and peaceful exchanges and trading with other nations.

Along the coasts spread the country's salt flats: they stretch from the Liaodong Peninsula to Hainan Island. China leads the world in salt production, its output accounting for one-fifth of the world total.

Off our coasts, the sea contains abundant fish and other ocean resources. The country produces large amounts of world-famous pearls. The pearls produced in Hepu County, Beihai, Guangxi are called *nanzhu* (South Pearls); they surpass the *dongzhu* (East Pearls) of Japan and *xizhu* (West Pearls) of Europe in terms of color, brightness, symmetry and smoothness.

Aquatic animal and plant life is cultivated on the low beaches of the country. The ocean bottom has rich mineral resources: the East China Sea and the South China Sea hold one of the greatest oil reserves in the world. The country also has a large reserve of titanic

The seaside city Qingdao

placer and zircon deposits. These are precious metals, having enormous commercial value. There are also manganese nodules in the deep sea.

The ocean tides contain enormous energy, but this energy has not yet been harnessed. In the future, tidal energy will be employed to produce huge amounts of electric power. The displacement of the Qiantang River Tide is as great as eight meters at its peak, so the huge energy in this flow has the potential to provide the nation with inexpensive electricity. The possibilities for the country to utilize the ocean's power for electricity generation are very favorable.

Complex and Varied Climate

Since the country's area is so extensive and the terrain so diverse, the climate is complex and varied.

The northern part of the country verges on the Arctic, giving the north of Heilongjiang Province a long winter and no summer. Most days, it is extremely cold and is covered with thick snow and ice. Temperatures as low as minus 50 degrees centigrade have been recorded in Mohe — a record for the country. The southern part of the country is situated south of the Tropic of Cancer, almost at the Equator. That is why Hainan Island has a long summer and no winter, with flowers blooming and grass growing all year long. The average temperature of the Xisha Islands is 26 degrees centigrade; it is one of the places recording the highest temperatures in the country. Most of the country lies in the temperate zone and experiences four distinct seasons. In January, the difference in temperature between Harbin and Guangzhou is over 33 degrees centigrade.

The regions of plateaus and hills far from the ocean have arid climates, with low precipitation and great temperature fluctuations. In the inland regions of the northwest, the temperature changes are pronounced. A ballad describes the inhabitants of this place as "wearing fur-lined jackets in the morning and gauze clothes in the afternoon, eating watermelon while sitting around the fireplace." The annual precipitation at the edge of the Tarim Basin is lower than 10 millimeters, and rain sometimes does not fall for several years. It is the driest place in the country. Although the Yunnan-Guizhou Plateau has a high elevation, it is situated close to the subtropical zone. Therefore, the region is spared both the winter's freezing temperatures and the intense heat of the summer, and the climate is like spring all year round. In the southwestern high-mountain region, from the foot of a mountain to its peak, the climate takes on a very pronounced change. While the peak is covered with white snow, grass is lush halfway up the mountain. Then, at the foot of the mountain, trees and flowers are blossoming - it is a tropical scene. The eastern coastal region has a moist climate and four distinct seasons because of its proximity to the ocean. The annual precipitation can reach as high as 1,600 millimeters. The annual precipitation of Huoshaoliao in Taiwan is over 6,000 millimeters: this is the highest average annual precipitation in the country.

Monsoons blowing from the temperate zone make the temperature of most parts of the country higher than in other places in the world at the same latitude, while the temperature in the winter is lower. The summer winds bring rainfall and warm temperatures, while the winter winds bring the aridity and cold from inland. These forces make the temperature differences between the south and the north even wider.

The greatly varied climate has provided an extremely rich variety of animal and plant life.

Abundance of Mineral Resources

The country is rich in mineral resources, possessing deposits of almost all known minerals. To date, deposits of 162 types of minerals have been discovered, with proven reserves of 148 of them. China is one of the few countries in the world that has been blessed with a near-complete list of minerals.

The country was the world's first to use coal. It has rich coal reserves and its coal mines may be found nearly everywhere. Total proven reserves have already reached over 900 billion tons. Shanxi Province is the country's key region for coal production. Trucks and trains continually send Shanxi's coal to domestic destinations and to ports for export to numerous other countries.

China has huge oil reserves: from the Northeast Plain, Bohai Bay, and the North China Plain to Hubei and Hunan Provinces in the south, large-scale oilfields have been established. The country is one of the largest oil producers in the world.

The Daqing Oilfield, the Shenli Oilfield in Northern China, the Bohai Oilfield, the South China Sea Oilfield, the Xingjiang Oilfield and others are all well known.

Oil wells on the plains and oil extraction platforms on the sea present one spectacular scene after another.

Natural gas production follows that of oil, and the country's gas reserves are also abundant. Proven natural gas reserves in the country have already reached 38 trillion cubic meters. Pipelines that wind thousands of kilometers take natural gas from underground to every part of the country, to be utilized for industrial or consumer consumption.

The nonferrous metal reserves of the country are also abundant. The proven reserves of metals like tungsten, antimony, lithium, tin, rare earth and titanium rank first in the world, and reserves of copper, aluminum, molybdenum, lead, mercury and nickel are in the front rank. These are all important raw materials for scientific and technological applications.

The country's iron ore reserves have reached 44 billion tons — one of the largest in the world.

The country also has huge deposits of uranium ore, rare in the world. These deposits provide important raw material for developing the country's nuclear power industry.

China's non-metal mineral resources are also abundant: over 4,300 locations produce these minerals. This too is rare in the world, and is a source of the country's pride.

The types of salt produced in the country include sea salt, well salt, pond salt and rock salt. The salt reserves in Cha'erhan Salt Lake in the Qaidam Basin alone are as much as 25 billion tons. This could supply the country for thousands of years.

The country's reserves of sulfuric iron ore, magnesite and boron ore rank first in the world; the reserves of phosphorite ranks second; the reserves of mica, asbestos, fluorite, bentonite, graphite, pyrophyllite, black lead, kaolin, pearlite and limestone are also in the front ranks. The reserves of Glauber's salt, natural alkali

A wine vessel with
an air of mystery

and feldspar are rich. China's marble, with its many varieties of design and colour, is famous all over the world.

Diamonds are the world's hardest matter, and natural diamond resources are rare nearly everywhere in the world. Diamond crystals are always very small, but in China, a large diamond, with a weight of 31.7572 grams, was discovered. This treasure is a world-class rarity.

"Vast in territory and rich in natural resources" is really an apt description of the country.

An Abundance of Rare and Unusual Fauna

On the country's vast land, oceans, rivers and lakes live countless rare birds and unusual animals.

Milu, or Père David's deer, is generally called *si bu xiang* ["Unlike Four": neither deer, horse, donkey, nor ox]. The giant panda, a precious animal unique to this country, is a national treasure. This is an animal that evolved over hundreds of thousands of years from a carnivore to one eating exclusively bamboo. It is indeed a rare "living fossil". The golden monkey is also a valued animal, unique to China. In addition, we have the mighty Amur tiger, and valiant tigers of other species in south China. The country boasts unique species like the white-fin dolphin and Chinese alligator in the Yangtze River. The extremely rare white bear lives in the thick forest of Shengnongjia in Hubei Province. Along the coasts of Xiamen and Qingdao, we also have a precious and ancient fish — the lancelet.

The country has over 1,000 types of birds, the vast majority of whom are valued and useful. Some of the more prized ones are the red ibis, the red-crowned crane, the mandarin duck, the white-comb long-tail pheasant, the golden pheasant, the lark, the yellow-waist sunbird, and the red-billed leiothrix. Pheasants like the crossoptilon mantchuricum, the blue eared pheasant and the white eared pheasant are extremely beautiful, but are found in few numbers.

The shame is that while human beings were busy with their own development, they plundered and destroyed the environments of other living things. A number of animals in the country are already facing extinction; among them are the white-fin dolphin, the giant panda, and the Amur tiger. Recently many people have started to realize that animals are our friends and should enjoy the same rights as do humans. Consequently, many nature preserves have been established to protect the giant panda and encourage its propagation, and to make the Amur tiger a proud species again. Some good results have been achieved, but there is a great deal more to be done.

Varied and Rare Flora

Upon China's vast land are countless species, including both rare trees and precious flowers and grasses. There are over 32,000 types of higher plants in China. There are 7,000 species of woody plants, of which 2,800 are species of trees: the number is only about 600 in North America, and 250 in Europe. Of the most ancient seed plants — gymnosperms — there are 13 families and over 700 species in the world, and China alone has 12 families and over 300 species. Among them are the ginkgo, cathaya

Jiuzhaigou, Sichuan

argyrophylla, dragon spruce and dawn redwood. These ancient trees are preserved in this country, but long extinct in other parts of the world. Many countries introduced them again from China in the 20th century. We also have the dove tree, eucommia, and Campotheca acuminaa [a garden plant believed to have cancer-curing properties] — all seed plants. Over 2,000 species of edible plants are found in China - there are only 1,000 species in Europe and America together.

In the Xishuangban'na region of Yunnan Province, there is an expanse of thick tropical rain forest — the only place in the world at the same latitude. Other such forests have long ago reverted to desert.

The dawn redwood lived in the early Cretaceous period of the Mesozoic Era, flourishing in East Asia, North America and Europe, but was thought to have become extinct in the fourth Ice Age; nothing was left but its fossils. However, in Sichuan and Hubei Provinces, over 1,000 dawn redwood trees were discovered in the 1940s. The trees were as tall as 35 meters with trunks up to 2.3 meters in diameter, and of graceful appearance; their discovery rocked the world of botany. The dawn redwood is called a "living fossil".

Seedlings were given to several countries in America and Europe to permit them to grow their own "living fossils".

In the Baiyin Aobao region of Inner Mongolia, there exists the only stand of dragon spruce in the world, about 5,000 trees. Many tourists from different countries and regions have traveled tens of thousands of kilometers to pay tribute to this green ancestor, and pick a few dried branches to take as souvenirs.

The dove tree, a beautiful ornamental tree, was thought to have become extinct a long time ago, but with the country's unique natural environment, it returned to prosperity in Guizhou, Hubei and Sichuan Provinces. When the flowers blossom, they look like a flock of doves nestling on the tree — that is why it is also called the "Chinese dove tree". To see this beautiful tree, one should go to the Shengnonjia forest region of Hubei Province, where vast numbers of dove trees grow.

Cathaya argyrophylla could be called the "giant panda of plant", or the "glacial old man". It had also been thought to have become extinct a long time ago, but now lives on in the southwestern region in China. Able to withstand the hardship of wind, frost, downpour and snow to live for generation after generation, it has become the pride of the country. Biologists worldwide are fascinated with it, for the plant provides them with a valuable opportunity to study the evolution of the Earth.

In some coastal areas in Fujian Province grow large expanses of mangrove. They are inundated when the tide rises, and fish and birds gambol in the branches. When the tide recedes, we see an expanse of fiery-red wood.

The country has even more rare flowers, grasses and medicinal herbs. The azalea, the primrose and the rough gentian are called the "three famous flowers", while the peony, also known as "the king of flowers", is also one of the country's special plants. The spring orchid and the autumn chrysanthemum have enjoyed the admiration of poets from ancient times; the freshness of the bamboo is always esteemed.

Ali Grassland, Tibet

Though the country has a vast collection of rare plants, in view of the huge population, there is little forested and green area. The forest coverage of China is 13.92%, less than that of most countries.

Many natural disasters originate from "human errors"; today, environmental protection has become the consensus. The nation is building shelter-forests in the northwest, growing grassy fields, stabilizing drifting sand, and otherwise protecting land and establishing water projects. Much has already been achieved by these efforts. Large areas of sand-covered land have sprouted green grass and large trees, denuded hills are becoming green again and forests are recovering and renewing their growth.

In 1999, Kunming, in Yunnan Province, hosted a grand global assembly — the World Expo of Flowers and Horticulture. This was not just a forum to show the world China's rare flowers, grasses, and horticultural traditions, and to welcome presentations on flowers and horticulture from representatives of other countries: It was an opportunity to build the host's and the attendees' collective consciousness on environmental protection to safeguard their respective homelands.

Temple of Heaven, Beijing

Long before the first human being was born on this planet, plants already thrived. They have the right to live on. All those flowers, grasses and trees that lived through the ancient and pleasant times should still beautify the lives of today. The freshness and the beauty of greenery should continue to live on and be enjoyed.

Natural Tourism Resources

China has rich natural resources to attract tourism.

One can enjoy the vast forests and white snow-covered slopes of the towering Changbai Mountain, where the Heaven Pond and the Pouring Fall can be found. Mount Tai in the east, Mount Hua to the west, Mount Song in the middle, Mount Heng to the south, and Mount Heng in the north are together called "the Five Sacred Mountains". The rareness of their steep slopes, beauty and

Gugong Palace
Theater, Beijing

magnificence present spectacles unmatched elsewhere in the world. In the Huangshan Mountains, strange-looking stones, a sea of clouds, rare pine trees and hot springs make visitors reluctant to leave. Lushan Mountain is a beautiful summer resort; Li Bai (a famous poet in the Tang Dynasty) wrote a poem glorifying its Xianglu Peak Falls: "Flowing straight down three thousand *chi*, as if the Milky Way is falling from the ninth sky". This poem alone makes that scene world-famous. Mount Emei, which is claimed to be the "most beautiful scene in the world", with its sequestered and delicate atmosphere, makes visitors feel as though they are in a fairyland.

There is also the beautiful Xishuangbanna, which is like an emerald, Guilin, whose "mountain and water scenes top the world", and the silvery coasts and white sands of Beihai. There are the coconut woods and orange seas of Sanya, Hainan Island. Suzhou and Hangzhou both claim to be "Paradise". Because of their serene and tasteful gardens, and the graceful and beautiful West Lake, visitors are reluctant to leave. Sun Moon Lake and Ali Mountain of Taiwan are also world-famous scenic attractions. The subterranean "Dragon Palace" in Guizhou intoxicates one's mind and heart, and the flood tide of the Qiantang River, with its massive swell and thunderous sound, makes watchers tremble.

The most spectacular city is the capital, Beijing: by climbing the Great Wall and visiting the Temple of Heaven, one can keenly feel the meaning of solemnity, grandeur and strength.

It is not possible to visit every corner of the land even in a lifetime, and a description of its vastness and beauty would more than fill a large book.

Chapter Two
A Multi-Ethnic Nation

—

Stories of the Origin of Man and the Nation

How are human beings born? How were the clans that we were born and grew up in formed? This is a question that people in every nation ask themselves. Every nation has its own stories of the origins of human beings and nations; these local legends and myths, together with those universally believed, come together to complete our beliefs of the creation of the world.

According to this country's legends and myths, all people were created by the original ancestor of mankind, the Great Mother, Nü Wa.

Pan Gu separated heaven and earth, but he lived, and died alone. The world before Pan Gu was a huge void; all of heaven and earth were empty, it seemed that time had stopped. Countless years passed; then the ancestor of mankind, Nü Wa appeared. She could not abide being alone, and was unwilling to let heaven and earth continue to be empty of living things. So she created the first human beings after her own image: she took some loess and shaped some "mud dolls" in her form, and set them on the land. A miracle happened: these "mud dolls" started moving as soon as they touched the ground. They moved

Left: A mural depicting people praying for harvest

47

their limbs, shook their heads, and opened their eyes to see this world. They opened their mouths to make sounds, and then they jabbered and laughed and ran around with leaps and bounds. They gathered around Nü Wa and cried in unison a sound of love — it was the most familiar sound - "Mama".

Seeing all these lives that she had created, Nü Wa felt very pleased, and continued creating them. She worked day in and day out. When she was tired, she just dipped the branch in mud and then touched the ground: the mud instantly turned into humans, who scattered in all directions.

Nü Wa mated men and women, so that they would breed children. Human beings then continued to multiply in this fashion.

In other legends of the Chinese nation, different nations are described as brothers and sisters. The Lisu people said, "three brothers circled a fire to cook bamboo; when the bamboo joint cracked, their sharp cries were all different. The first son said '*ma chi*', the second son said '*a jian zhi zhe*', and the third son, '*a la ye*'". So we have the languages for the Han, the Yi, and the Lisu. Some said, at the time of the Great Flood, the people all hid in a large gourd. When the gourd floated onto dry land, 100 men walked out of it: They were the forefathers of the Han, Dai, Lisu, Jingpo, Bai and Hui peoples. The Tibetan and the Dong nationalities also have similar legends, only the gourd is sometimes an egg. In Hani's legend, Nü Wa became Ta Po Ran; humans were not formed by her, but were given birth from her stomach - she gave birth to over 70 babies. In order to distinguish them, Nü Wa gave them different names: Hani, Yi, Dai, Bai, Han.... The legend of the ethnic group Xi Men Va is also interesting: the first person that walked from the large gourd was "Yan Va", the ancestor of today's Va nationality; the second was called "Ni Wen", the ancestor of today's Bai nationality; the third "San Mu Dai", the ancestor of today's Dai nationality; and the fourth, "Sai Ke", the ancestor of

A colored earthen pot with reliefs of nudes

the Han nationality. All in all, the 56 ethnic groups of the Chinese nation are brothers with the same mother. Even in antediluvian legends, all are blood brothers.

The Chinese account for one-fifth of the world's population. For different reasons, many Chinese people now live abroad or have taken up a foreign nationality. No matter where in the world, one can always see descendants of Hua Xia.

=

The Origin of
the Ancient Ancestors

Anthropologists, or course, do not regard the myth of Nü Wa creating mankind as having any scientific foundation. According to research, the oldest

**Mysterious
human faces**

direct ancestor of mankind was Ramapithecus. This ape-like creature lived about 14 million years ago. Fossils of Ramapithecus have been found both in India and East Africa. That is why anthropologists deduce that all ancestors of man are descendants of ancient African apes, and the human race made its way to all parts of the world from the African continent.

In 1985, English geneticists researched the kinship of races by examining their DNA; the result was that DNA samples from 26 Chinese ethnic groups were found to be similar to those of Africans. At the same time, the DNA of the indigenous Maoris of New Zealand and the Bohemians were found to be similar to that of most Chinese ethnic groups. This means that they also are descendants of Chinese, who traveled across the oceans.

Some anthropologists assert that it is likely that there were two kinds of primitive man. One had its origin in Africa and set foot to the rest of world; the other group was born in numerous other countries and regions, like China, then migrated to other places, like New Zealand and other Oceanian regions. So it appears that the place of origin of mankind is probably not just Africa, but could be many other places too.

In 1956 and 1975, the fossils of ancient apes that lived at the same time as did Ramapithecus were found in Kaiyuan City and Lufen County of Yunnan Province. This means this land fostered the earliest ancestors of mankind.

Ramapithecus was able to walk erect and use natural clubs and stones to hunt for foods. It dug plants' rhizomes, but was not able to make tools. Therefore, it is called an anthropoid, or "man-ape".

After many years of evolution, about two to three million years ago, a tool-making creature appeared. However, the characteristics of ancient apes were still evident; that is why it was called "ape" or "ape-man", (scientific name "Homo Erectus"). This ape was widely dispersed across China. From the fossils of these apes, Yuanmou Man, Lantian Man and Peking Man were identified.

On November 3 1998, the Xinhua News Agency of China announced that Chinese archaeologists had discovered 180 stone implements made in ancient times, together with many fossils of primates, in Lali Hill, Suncun Town, Fanchang County of Anhui Province. Although fossils of man were not found, the unearthed stone implements confirmed that mankind lived in this region approximately 2 to 2.4 million years ago — much earlier than had been previously recorded.

The fossils of Yuanmou Man were excavated in Yuanmou County, Yunnan Province. They lived about 1.7 million years ago. These are the earliest erect-standing apes ever found in Asia.

A pot topped with a human-head-shaped closure

The fossils of Lantian Man were found in Lantian County, Shaanxi Province. They lived around 800,000 years ago.

Compared to them, Peking Man, who lived around 500,000 years ago, is much more recent. The fossils of Peking Man were found in the caverns of Longgu Hill, Zhoukoudian, southwest of Beijing. On December 2, 1929, China's archaeologists and anthropologists discovered a complete cranium fossil. This news created a huge ripple in anthropological and archaeological circles.

In accordance with excavated cranium fossil, a likeness of Peking Man was reconstructed. The forehead was low and flat, two thick and large eyebrow bones ran along the upper edges of the eye sockets, and the skull was thick. The shape of the skull was large in the lower part, tapering to a smaller crown, and the chin jutted forward. It showed many of the characteristics of the ancient apes. But the upper limbs of the Peking Man were similar to those of modern man; this means that Peking Man was already working with both hands, which are basically the same as those of modern man.

Regrettably, the original cranium fossil of Peking Man disappeared during the Japanese invasion of China. Its whereabouts are still unknown. This precious relic of mankind's history is lost somewhere. Maybe it is calling in an unseen world, and is longing to get back to its homeland.

The social life of Peking Man appears to represent the earliest developed social phase of human history. Now, over 40 remains of Peking Man have been excavated, in addition to numerous started but not completely finished stone implements, and horn and bone implements. In the caverns of Longgu Hill, there is a layer of ash as thick as six meters containing fish bones, animal bones and seeds: this means that Peking Man had learned to use fire. When fire was first carried into the cold, wet and gloomy cavern, what a giant step mankind had made toward the development of civilization!

Now, when one stands at the entrance to the caverns in Longgu Hill, one can appreciate how long and difficult a road had been traveled, lighted by flame. History lies directly below; this feeling could only be made real when standing in the capital, Beijing.

When the leaping flames rose with a crackling noise and lighted the dark sky, everything around the cavern was painted with a flashing colour, now bright and now dark, how mysterious, strange and awe-inspiring it must been! How could they not dance and shout around the fire, while calling out their longings, fears and happiness? Now, there are still many societies who worship fire, and the ceremony of joyously singing and dancing around a fire is still intoxicating.

After Peking Man, there was Mabei Man (excavated in Mabei County,

Shaoguan, Guangdong Province) who lived 100,000 years ago, Changyang Man (excavated in Changyang County, Hubei Province), and Dingcun Man (excavated in Dingcun, Xiangfeng County, Shanxi Province). These "men" are closer to modern men, and academics refer to them as early period Homo Sapiens. For example, the teeth of Dingcun Man look very much like present-day Chinese, most of whom belong to the modern Mongoloid race.

Ancestors wearing clothing made of tree leaves

During the period from about 40,000 to 50,000 years ago, there was a development from early period Homo Sapiens to later period Homo Sapiens. The fossils of later period Homo Sapiens found in China include the Hetao Man in Inner Mongolia, Liujiang Man in Liujiang, Guangxi Province, Upper Cave Man in the upper caves in Longgu Hill, Beijing and Ziyang Man in Ziyang, Sichuan Province. The Upper Cave Man had learned how to make fire by artificial means.

China's ancient legends have passed down interesting and cherished accounts of this era. Legend has it that several outstanding figures appeared in China's primitive clans: Youchao Shi, Suiren Shi, Fuxi Shi and Shennong Shi.

Shennong Shi who tasted all kinds of herbs

Youchao Shi taught people how to build homes atop trees. Suiren Shi taught people how to make fire by drilling wood. Fuxi Shi was even greater — he taught people how to weave nets and catch fish, how to make earthenware to cook fish, shrimp and meat. He taught people how to raise livestock. He also invented the Eight Trigrams [eight combinations of three whole or broken lines], and used them in further combinations, resulting in the creation of 64 patterns which function to explain changes in the natural environment, and to divine and record events. As a matter of fact, the Eight Trigrams were created by people in later periods, and it is only the legend that attributes their invention to Fuxi Shi.

The contributions of Shennong Shi were even greater. He tasted all kinds of herbs, told people which plants were edible, which had curative properties and which were poisonous. Without him, today's rich collection of edible plants and medicinal herbs would not exist — of course, this is legend again. He also taught people how to farm, and effected the great transition from the traditional practice of herding and hunting to the era of domestication of animals.

Fuxi Shi, Shennong Shi and Nü Wa are together called the Three Sage Rulers. The saying, "From the time of Pan Gu separating heaven and sky, the era of the Three Sage Rulers and Five Virtuous Emperors until now", has become the most commonly known shorthand to describe the history of the Chinese nation.

≡

The Formation and Development of the Chinese Nation

The Chinese nation is a large and harmonious family, with 56 brothers and sisters. This large family was formed over a period of time by the fusion of different ethic groups into the Chinese nation. The most populous of them — the Han — was itself formed by the fusion of different nations.

There were three eras in China's history that saw the greatest fusion of groups: the era of the Spring and Autumn Period and the Warring States Period; the era of the Wei, Jin, and Southern and Northern Dynasties; and finally, the Yuan Dynasty.

The Yellow Emperor's tribe and the Red Emperor's tribe continually merged with surrounding tribes, forming the Yellow and Red Tribe. This tribe then combined with different tribes in the Central Plain and the middle reaches of the Yellow River to form

the earliest Hua Xia nation. After over 500 years of war, assimilation and fusion
during the Spring and Autumn Period and the Warring States Period up to the time of
Qin and Han Dynasties, the main body of the Chinese nation, the Han, was formed.
This was accomplished by assimilating other tribes. When the Jiuli Tribe with its leader
Ciyou were growing in the southeast, they also merged with many local tribes, forming
ethnic groups living today in China's southern region.

In the period of Han dynasty, the contact with different groups in the Western
Regions and with minority ethnic groups in the southwest was ongoing. These
nations gradually became integrated into the larger family of China. During the
same period there were constant wars with the Hun in the north. Later, a large
number of the northern Huns migrated westward and gradually settled in Europe.
Some Huns migrated southward, and settled in the region near the Great Wall.
Wang Zhaojun of the Han Dynasty married Shanyu, a Hun leader. The marriage
facilitated communication between the Han and his faction of the Huns.

In the period of Wei, Jin, and Southern and Northern Dynasties, different
ethnic groups in the north — the Xianbei, Qiang, Jie and Di migrated inland into
the Yellow River Valley, settling with the Han, and were gradually becoming fused
into the Han ethnic group.

After the great integration in Wei, Jin and Southern and Northern Dynasties,
the Tang Dynasty marked the apogee of the country's ancient history: many
different ethnic groups lived together harmoniously. Princess Wencheng married
Songtsam Gambo, king of Tubo (ancient name for Tibet), and this effected close
relations between the Tibetan regime and the Tang Dynasty.

During the Song Dynasty, the Han constantly waged war with the Qidan
and Nü Zhen clans in the north, but finally, both became members of the larger
family of ethnic groups.

The Yuan Dynasty marked the end of the era of warring regimes which had
lasted for over 300 years since the Five Dynasties Period. Different ethnic groups

"Sedan chair"
(by Yan Liben,
Tang Dynasty)

administering separate domains were finally replaced by a state regime. The large-scale resettlement of ethnic groups continued, as ethnic minority groups migrated into the Central Plains and the Han continued to shift to the border areas where minority groups lived. This created a phase of cooperation in the integration of the different ethnic groups into the Yuan Dynasty's domain, and accelerated the process of fusion. Tibet became a formal administrative district of the Yuan Dynasty, and the Tibetan people became members of the larger family of China. The Yuan Dynasty also set up the Penghu Islands Inspection Bureau and brought Taiwan and Penghu into its domain. As a result, the domain of the Yuan Dynasty was larger than that of any of the preceding dynasties. At the same time, the Yuan Dynasty built a multi-ethnic country.

The process of integrating the nation was also very brisk during Ming and Qing Dynasties. Under the reign of Emperor Kangxi, a multi-ethnic and unified domain was firmly established, with the different ethnic groups of the Chinese nation living together harmoniously.

The formation of the large family of the Chinese nation was the result of developments in the Chinese history, and of the fruit of different ethnic groups integrating into one. Every ethnic group, with its own customs and culture, integrated with one another and formed a unified Chinese culture.

Chapter Three

The Long and Brilliant History of China

Carved marks on
a tortoise shell from
8000 years ago

One day in 1899, Wang Yirong, Chancellor of the Directorate of Education of the Qing Dynasty, was examining a pile of Chinese herbal medicine. He suddenly noticed something unusual: zigzag marks and curious carvings on some pieces of so-called "dragon bones" caught his attention. The marks looked like some kind of symbols. Wang perhaps did not realize what had happened at that moment — Fate had placed in his hand one key to the mystery of Chinese civilization. Further studies by Wang suggested that those marks on the dragon bones were ancient Chinese characters — oracle bone inscriptions — records of events that had transpired more than 3,000 years before.

Tortoise shells and flat animal bones were employed by the kings of the Shang Dynasty (1700-1027 BC) in divination. Approximately 150,000 of these pieces have been discovered. The inscriptions on the bones were mainly records of events and social activities such as sacrifices, battles and wars, hunts, agriculture, animal husbandry and geography. These recordings have been the most important contributions to the study of the Shang Dynasty. The oracle bone inscriptions shed light on ancient Shang society, and serve as evidence of the existence of the legendary Shang Dynasty more than three millennia ago. These findings have dated the history of China much earlier than had been recorded up to that time, and illuminate the brilliance of the Chinese civilization that dawned thousands of years before the Shang Dynasty.

Left: A white
earthen vessel of
Longshan Culture of
the Neolithic Age

—

The Dawn of
Chinese Civilization

Just when the Chinese civilization first emerged and how many millennia it has endured still remains a mystery. Conventional belief is that Chinese civilization has lasted for five thousand years, but this belief is based on legendary figures such as Yao and Shun. Legends surrounding them portray a transition from a matrilineal society to a patrilineal one. Many of China's legends and lore illustrated this preliminary stage of Chinese civilization.

The War between Yan Huang (Red and Yellow Emperors) and Chi You

In prehistoric times, tribes and clans roamed the vast plains along the mighty Yellow and Yangtze Rivers. Legend has it that in the northwest, a beautiful girl from the Youjiao tribe by the name of Fu Bao was married to the chieftain of another clan, Shao Dian. One day Fu Bao witnessed lightning circling the seven stars of the Big Dipper and illuminating the whole world. As a result, she conceived. Twenty-five months later, she gave birth to a baby boy. Because the boy grew up by the Ji River and resided on Xuanyuan Mountain, he replaced his surname with Ji, and later called himself Xuanyuan. Folklore relates that he became known and worshipped as Yellow Emperor (Huang Di), one of the forefathers of Chinese civilization.

Yellow Emperor,
the forefather of
Chinese civilization

As the leader of his tribe, the Yellow Emperor engaged himself and his followers in hard work and growth. He implemented enlightened rules based on virtue. He educated his people to be literate and civil. Agricultural practices progressed, expertise and techniques were acquired and perfected in such crafts such as digging wells, making mortars and pestles, arches and arrows, taming oxen, bridling horses, driving carts, building canoes and boats. His wife, Lei Zu, taught the people to raise silk worms and spin silk, to dye cloth and linen, to tailor garments and make footwear. Cang Jie, the scribe of Yellow Emperor, invented Chinese characters. Da Nao, the astronomer, charted the movements of the sun and moon and designed the Celestial Stems and Terrestrial Branches calendar system. Ling Lun, Yellow Emperor's court musician, made innovations in musical instruments. These efforts and advances enabled the Yellow Emperor's tribe to lead others in the development of culture and civilization.

With its ever-expanding power, the tribe gradually merged and assimilated with many smaller clans and factions in the surrounding areas. Its center moved step by step from its original homeland in north Shaanxi to the middle Yellow River area. It extended still farther to the east until it finally settled near Zhuolu in modern-day Heibei Province.

About the same time that the Yellow Emperor's tribe entered the mid- and lower regions of the Yellow River, western tribes led by the Red Emperor and the Jiu Li ethnic group from the south were also advancing into the same region.

It is said that the tribe led by the Red Emperor (Yan Di) developed by the River Jiang to the east of Qishan in Shaanxi. It later migrated eastward, down the River Wei and entered the southwestern part of Henan, before arriving finally in what is today's Shandong Province. The Red Emperor, also a son of Shao Dian and so a younger brother of the Yellow Emperor, bore the surname of Jiang and had as his epithet Shen Nong. Said to have been born with an ox's head and a human body, the Red Emperor is also worshipped as one of China's forefathers.

Another legendary figure in Chinese folklore is Chi You — he was the leader of the Jiu Li tribe in the south. Legend has it that the tribe invented the technique for smelting copper. Its level of civilization was higher than that of the Yellow Emperor's and the Red Emperor's tribes.

The Jiu Li tribe pushed northward. When trying to enter the mid- and lower stretches of the Yellow River, it encountered the Red Emperor's forces, who were making their home in the the region known today as Shandong. The two sides engaged in battle. Defeated, the Red Emperor turned to the Yellow Emperor for help. The united forces checked the advance of Chi You, but were not able to conquer him.

A decisive war followed between the allied forces of the Yellow Emperor and the Red Emperor against those of Jiu Li tribesmen on Zhuolu Plain. The two sides faced one another in a stalemate for a long time before a fierce battle finally erupted. Soldiers and warriors from both sides fought with weapons made of copper, wood and stone in fierce bloodletting. It was a grueling battle. According to legend, the divinities of the wind, thunderstorms and drought were invoked to assist in the fighting, filling the field and sky with fog, dust, gusts of wind and pouring rain. The Yellow Emperor had devised the compass, aiding his forces in orienting themselves in the battle. The battle ended with the defeat and death of Chi You, as well as the disintegration of his tribe. Some of Chi You's tribesmen followed the Yellow and Red Emperors. These were assimilated into one ethnic group, the Hua Xia people. Others fled farther south and are the antecedents of the ethnic minorities in south China today. Some escaped onto the high seas, prompting some anthropologists to suggest that the Maoris and American Indians may be the descendants of these early Chinese who abandoned their homeland. This remains, however, only a hypothesis.

Yu, the Great Tamer of Floods

One of the best-known leaders of the tribal coalition after the Yellow and Red Emperors was Yao. During his reign, the mighty Yangtze River overflowed and inundated the plains, burying everything in its way under water and waves. Yao designated Gun, leader of the Xia tribe, to oversee efforts to stem the floods. The Xia tribe was of the Yellow Emperor's family and the chieftain, Gun, was the great grandson of Xuanyuan — the Yellow Emperor.

Gun tried to contain the floods by building dikes to check and stop the water from overflowing. But after nine years conditions were even worse. Floods were more frequent and the land was inundated in all directions,.

Muddy water destroyed people's shelters and rendered them homeless and desperate.

When Yao became too old to preside over things, he passed his title and authority as the head of the tribal coalition to Shun. The decision was approved by a conference of elders. This was the so-called *Shan Rang*, or abdication in favor of another person with virtue. Upon ascension, Shun toured and inspected the land. He was shocked at the degree of destruction brought by the floods. He ordered the detention of Gun in Yu Shan, and later sentenced him to death in order to pacify the anger and outrage of the men and women of the tribes. Shun went on to assign Yu, son of Gun, to take up the task of taming the floods.

Following in his father's steps, Yu was determined to save his tribesmen from the ravages of the floods. He led his men down the Yangtze River and up the Yellow River, leaving footprints all along Huai and Ji Rivers. He and his men went far and wide, observing closely the movements of the water and the geographic surroundings. Yu came to realize that Gun had failed beacause he had been trying to contain the water. He decided to abandon this approach in favor of letting the water flow and ebb in its natural course. So he and his men began to dredge and scour the riverbeds, sweeping away the blockages, building and strengthening dikes where necessary, and draining stagnant water from the lowlands. They worked only with tools made of wood and stone in this large-scale and difficult undertaking.

During the thirteen years Yu preoccupied himself with this task, he even bypassed his home trice without visiting. In the end, his efforts paid off. Floods subsided and the plains returned to life. Yu went on to order Houji to distribute seed grain to the people and teach them how to farm. Peace and prosperity were recovered.

Yu's contributions in harnessing the deluge and encouraging farming were well-recognized by his tribesmen. He was elected leader of the tribal coalition to succeed Shun. Since he was born in the Xia clan, he was also known as Xia Yu, and is venerated as Yu the Great.

Historical records and archaeological findings have confirmed that the Xia Dynasty was the first regime in China, beginning approximately 4000 years ago, and Yu was its first ruler.

In 1981, earthenware pieces with abstract marks were unearthed in the Yangjiawan relic site in Yichang, Hubei. Should these abstract carvings prove to be early characters, China's civilization would date 1000 years earlier than previously thought, to claim a history of 6000 years.

In 1983, in Wuyang, Henan, carved marks were again discovered. Some experts believe that those symbols, dating back 7000 years, were the precursors to oracle bone inscriptions. If this is true, then China's recorded history could have begun more than 7000 years ago.

Discoveries unearthed in the Chahai ancient cultural relic site in Fuxin, Liaoning Province, one of the representative sites of the Hongshan Culture, pushed China's recorded history back even earlier, to 8000 years.

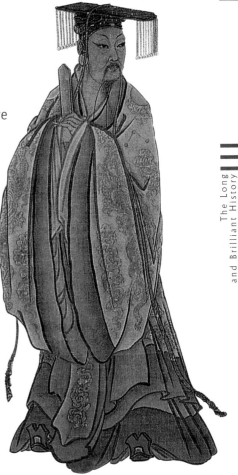

Yu the Great, founder of the Xia Dynasty

In 1993, Chinese archaeologists working on the site of the future Three Gorges Dam, discovered a rich collection of ancient cultural relics on Zhongbao Island in the Yangtze River. The remains recovered range from the prehistoric Neolithic Age dating back 6000 years, to those of the Xia, Shang, Zhou, Qin, Han, Tang, Song, Yuan, Ming and Qing Dynasties - almost an underground general history exhibition of China. The strata coincide precisely with the demarcations by Chinese historians of the dynasties and periods, serving as powerful evidence of the credibility of historical recordings.

No matter how historians might interpret these findings in the future, we can conclude with certainty now that China has a long history, at least 5000 years old.

**A jade eagle:
the most ancient
in China**

An Overview of
the Evolution of
Chinese History

Like a meandering and gushing river, the history of China has clearly experienced ups and downs, rapids, and reverse flows. Let us take a brief look of the thousands of years of history.

About five to six thousand years ago, peoples living in various parts of China evolved one after another into thriving matrilineal societies. Approximately four to five thousand years ago those tribes and clans went on to organize themselves along patriarchal lines.

The Pre-Qin Period

It has been related that in 2000 BC, the Xia Dynasty, first in China's history, was established by Yu. Qi, son of Yu, succeeded his father and assumed power. This hereditary succession replaced the practice of abdication and passing on power in accordance with public consensus, marking the end of the legendary golden age of primitive society.

The practice of slavery emerged in the Xia Dynasty. The country was divided into nine administrative regions which were ruled by commissioned officers instead of by the top ruler's kinsmen. Laws were promulgated, and armed forces and courts were institutionalized.

Workmen in Xia had grasped the techniques of casting bronze vessels. Findings at the Erlitou cultural relic site in Henan, central China, prove the existence of bone instrument workshops and pottery kilns. Wine had been brewed in Xia — this fact serves as further evidence that manufacturing and agriculture industries had developed to some extent.

The Xia Dynasty, lasting more than 400 years, saw 14 generations of rulers and the reigns of 17 kings. History records that the 17th and last king of Xia, by the name of Jie, was a notorious despot.

Another tribe, led by their leader Tang, dethroned Jie and his regime and established the Shang Dynasty. During the reign of Pan Geng, Shang moved its capital to Yin (today's Xiaodun village, Anyang in Henan Province). Before finally settling there, Shang had shifted its center of control several times; this vacillation was detrimental to the development of the economy. After settling in at Yin, the Shang Dynasty experienced a period of peace and prosperity, representing the first economic and cultural boom in China's history. The Shang regime at Yin created and displayed a blaze of color in its cultural achievements — Shang was the leading civilization in the world of its time. Excavations at the buried Shang capital, Yin, started in 1928. Countless treasures, including bronze objects, jade and cut-stone work, ivory carvings and shell coins, were unearthed. These relics help to shed light on what that bustling and booming town of Yin might have looked like more than 3000 years ago.

One might imagine seeing on the broad, barren land, the erection of earthen copper smelters standing in a row. What a wild and exciting picture it must have been: the ovens continued to be fired day and night, and the horizon glowed in red. Since one crucible had a capacity of smelting only 12.7 kilos of copper at a time, many ovens and furnaces had to be fired simultaneously to cast one giant *ding*. A *ding* is an ancient cooking, and later a sacrificial, vessel, with two looped handles and three or four legs. It was a great undertaking to cast a giant *ding*, with hundreds of slaves working together to the beat and rhythm of their hoarse and resonant shouting. The liquid, molten copper must have made a sizzling sound as it gushed into the sand molds amidst engulfing flames. At the first ray of sunrise the next morning, a prodigious bronze *ding* would be found standing in a barren field. The largest one unearthed so far is the Simuwu *ding*: it weighs 875 kilos and stands 1.33 meters tall. Producing a *ding* like this would be a very challenging effort even today, let alone more than 3000 years ago.

The Shang Dynasty led the world in its time in such areas as metallurgy, agriculture and animal husbandry. The development of its system of barter and commerce was one of the most advanced in the world, and the exchange of commodities reached as far as the China's southeastern coastlines. The many copper coins found in Yin ruins were probably the earliest metal currencies in the world. When the Shang regime was later replaced with that of Zhou, the new regime continued to encourage the trade of commodities between regions. Those who specialized in trade were referred to as "Shang folks", or merchants. Some historians believe that the concept of merchants, commerce, shops and

Right: An ancient square wine vessel

commodities (all beginning with the character for "*shang*" in modern Chinese) originated in the exchange trade the Shang people practiced during the Zhou Dynasty.

The creation of the oracle bone inscriptions was a great contribution of the Shang Dynasty. The people of Shang designed the Celestrial Stems and Territorial Branches to register the days and years. In this calendar system, sixty years make a circle called Jiazi. Each year has twelve months, and the leap year thirteen. This calendar, in its time, was quite scientific and served its intended purpose quite well.

Disciplined choral music troupes were also organized in the Shang Dynasty. They staged beautiful performances.

There were all together thirty kings in the reign of the Shang Dynasty.

King Wen and King Wu of Zhou jointly established the Western Zhou (11th century BC-771 BC). The system of slavery developed to a higher level in this period. A complete and intricate bureaucratic system was devised and implemented. Metallurgy and agriculture advanced, and silk spinning and dying techniques were ahead of their time.

At the time, the country bristled with small kingdoms and fiefs. Although the king of Zhou was honored as the Common Ruler, his authority extended to no more than the small, central patch of land under his direct rule. That piece of land was named the Central Kingdom, for it was the central capital and the symbol of the top authority. Since land and related titles were the object of much contention among the smaller leaders, the Central Kingdom (中国) gradually became the name of the country.

The Western Zhou later moved its capital to Luoyi (to the west of today's Luoyang, Henan Province). Named the Eastern Zhou Dynasty (770BC-256BC) by historians, it consisted of the Spring and Autumn Period (770BC-476BC) and the Warring States Period (475BC-221BC).

The two periods paved the way for the unity and prosperity of the Qin and Han Dynasties in later ages.

1. Advances in productivity laid a solid foundation for a later economic boom.

Houyi, the forebear of Zhou, was an expert in agriculture. His tribesmen were all skilled in farming, and agriculture was greatly advanced in Zhou. During the nearly 800 years from early Western Zhou to the end of Warring States Period, farming was the mainstay of the economy of central China. Many kinds of crops were cultivated: they were generally referred to as *Baigu*, or "A Hundred Grains". Metallurgy was developed to meet the demands of supplying farming tools and weapons. Ironware emerged in late Western Zhou period. Toward the end of the Spring and Autumn Period, a smelting technique was invented for making pig iron. The emergence of iron metallurgy and iron tools represented a great leap in technology and productivity. It made it possible to farm large pieces of arable land and induced the separation of handicraft industries from that of agriculture. These factors helped to dissolve the old social economic system based on slavery, and replaced it gradually with a feudal one. The advancement of the textile industry, including dyeing techniques, made possible further improvements in the people's economic status.

All in all, without the progress made during the Spring and Autumn and Warring States Period in metallurgy, agriculture, textile and trade, it would not have been possible for the economy during the Qin and Han Dynasties to prosper.

2. Political developments

A myriad of small fiefdoms and principalities existed in the early Zhou Dynasty, giving to continued conflicts. This division served as background and preparation for the mainstream political idea of ultimately unifying the country in the Qin and Han Dynasties. The dukes and princes of Zhou were effectively rulers of their fiefdoms, and had under them a hierarchy of ministers, secretaries and clerks. The aristocracy was also divided into the five grades of prince, marquis, earl, viscount and baron. Under the central authority there were such positions as Grand Preceptor and Grand Guardian (both assisting the Common Ruler with general state affairs), Minister of Agriculture, Minister of Public Works, Minister of War, the Grand Scribe, who was in charge of astronomy and history, and the Grand Diviner, overseeing religious and sacrificial rituals. This administrative structure and experience were later borrowed by the Qin and Han rulers.

3. Preparation in ideology and philosophy

The Spring and Autumn and Warring States Periods were also one of the periods in the Chinese history in which culture and ideology were most liberal and active. It was a time when basic important questions and values were resolved, in this early stage of the development of Chinese civilization. Debate was lively over various questions, schools of thought, methodologies and strategies. These dynamic clashes and arguments in contemporary thought pushed the ancient Chinese philosophy and culture to an unprecedented animation. The Confucianism of Kong Zi (Confucius), the Daoism of Lao Zi, the Universal Love of Mo Zi, or the Legalism of Hanfei Zi, all later became the principal sources of the Chinese culture.

Philosophy, especially the ideas concerning society and virtues, constituted the theoretical foundation for the ruling classes' reign and administration. The hundred schools of thought contending with one another during the Spring and Autumn and Warring States Periods had explored and established the theoretical bases for the strength and power of the later Qin and Han Dynasties.

Karl Jaspers once put forward the theory that around 500 BC there appeared in human history a pivotal age of culture. Four of the surviving ancient civilizations of the world, based on their separate experiences and interpretations of the world, raised metaphysical questions (questions beyond the bounds of time and space) as well as their own respective ways of solving problems, thus shaping the mentality of the each of these four civilizations. Jaspers thought these four cultures all came up with the same questions, though their answers differed from one to another. He said that modern civilization has been influenced by the extension, development and adaptations of these questions and answers. One of his "pivotal ages of culture" was the Spring and Autumn and Warring States Periods. It is not difficult to see that the Chinese culture being fostered at that time was an important source of influence on world civilization.

The Qin and Han Period

The Qin and Han periods witnessed the first flowering of Chinese civilization.

Yingzheng, king of Qin, one of seven states in the Warring States period, was a man of high political caliber, and a military strategist. He was determined to implement reforms and to build the military power of his country. In 221 BC, he succeeded in conquering the other six states and uniting central China. This first great empire was unprecedented in its vastness. It started the legally constituted authority of feudalism in China, which lasted for the next 2,100 years.

Yingzheng of Qin was the first to set a goal of unification and the first one to accomplish it. He wanted to challenge the orthodoxy that had gone before him. It is fair to say that the legally constituted feudal rule was put in place by Yingzheng,

A painting depicting Zhang Qian's mission to the Western Regions

and he left behind a deep impression as emperor and ruler. Few feudal kings and emperors were not cruel, fiery-tempered, or covetous. However, an overall, balanced historical evaluation should be given to each of them based on their contributions in long-term historical terms. Yingzheng rationalized the system of Chinese characters and weights and measures, and built roads and canals. He constructed the Great Wall. The name "*Qin ren*", or "citizens of Qin", was known throughout the neighboring regions. In some countries, people still call the Chinese "*Qin ren*" (actually, the name "China" may have been derived from "Qin"). Although the Qin Dynasty lasted for only a short time and was overthrown by the peasant uprising led by Cheng Sheng and Wu Guang, it laid the foundation of prosperity for the Han Dynasty.

The Han Dynasty is historically divided into the Western and Eastern Han Dynasties. The former lasted from 206 BC to 8 AD. Ending in a farmer's rebellion, the authority of Western Han was carried on by Liu Xiu, one of the kinsmen of the Han royal family. His army defeated all the other warlords and rebuilt the Han administration in Luoyang, beginning the Eastern Han Dynasty. It lasted almost two hundred years, from 25 AD to 220 AD.

Emperor Liu Xiu was one of the few rulers in the Chinese history who brought a dying Dynasty back to life. Under his reign, the civil administration and the military forces were both restored to good order. Although it made great contributions to China's history, the Eastern Han Dynasty failed to repeat the strength and prosperity of the Western Han Dynasty.

An eavestile glorifying the unity of Han

Because the Han Dynasty was built upon the ashes of the Qin, overthrown in the peasant rebellion, the early rulers implemented no harsh policies. They cut back the levies and the corvées and let the people catch their breath. Thus the social economic situation began to recover and progress into a healthy cycle. So when Liu Che, or Emperor Wu, the fifth emperor of the Dynasty, ascended the throne, the Dynasty was in full flower. He made great achievements in virtually every aspect — political, economic, cultural, ethnic harmony or foreign trade.

The major feats of Emperor Wu could be summarized as follows:

Politically, he further weakened the power of the nobility and cracked down on them by splitting their regional forces. He strengthened and consolidated the central authority begun by the Qin. His methods of manipulating and consolidating the power of the central administration, reforming personnel management and recruitment and refining the promotion system became a model for and were copied by kings and rulers in later ages.

Economically, he reformed the currency system and encouraged commerce. Many irrigation projects were completed to bolster agricultural production. Salt production and the iron industry were monopolized to increase state revenues.

This unprecedented economic power enabled the emperor to exhibit his prowess and wield his great army far and wide.

He led three major wars against the Hun horsemen warriors on the northern border. His victories helped to consolidate a country of multiple ethnic backgrounds, and to strengthen his hold on the northern territories.

In Sino-foreign relationships, Emperor Wu was a pioneer. He dispatched Zhang Qian as his emissary to Central Asia in order to built good relationships with the nomads. From then on, links were established with East Asia, Central Asia, West Asia and even North Africa. Silk and textiles were sent on an export route starting from Chang'an, the capital of China, to the Mediterranean, and even to Alexandria, Egypt. The Silk Road, stretching more than 7000 kilometers, brought China and Europe together. The sound of camel bells and galloping horses once rang through the sky of the desert, the poplars and rolling mountain ranges. The Silk Road opened the eyes of people in the East, and travelers brought back exotic specialties and vivid accounts of their travels. It enabled the dissemination of the relatively more advanced Chinese civilization to Central and Western Asia, and onward to Europe. It contributed much to the development of world civilization and east-west cultural exchanges.

The Western Han Dynasty saw the birth of Sima Qian, a great historian, man of letters and thinker. He created the impressive *Shi Ji*, or *Historical Records*, presented as a series of biographies. His book includes precise and vivid accounts of his age and the history of his time. His stylish prose inspired many men of letters. Sima Qian wielded his pen to record only the truth, with no apologies. His honest and straightforward approach to writing history was upheld by later historians as a model. Sima Qian presented unique and outstanding ideas in the fields of economics, military science, culture and politics.

Toward the end of the Western Han Dynasty, Buddhism was introduced into China. During the Eastern Han Dynasty, Cai Lun improved paper-making methods, and Zhang Heng invented a mobile celestial globe and an instrument to observe earthquakes. Doctors such as Zhang Zhongjing and Hua Tuo took the science of medicine to new heights and made it a respectable discipline. These were all great achievements.

The civilization of the Han Dynasty was so brilliant that it left indelible impressions on history. "Han" became the name of the majority Chinese ethnic group, representing most Chinese. In the Chinese language, the terms "the Chinese language" and "Sinology" both begin with the Chinese character for "Han". The word is also used by the world to refer to some of the important aspects of Chinese civilization. The influence of the Han Dynasty has indeed spread far and wide.

The Wei and Jin Periods

China was in the throes of war during the the Wei, Jin and the Northern and Southern Dynasties (220-581 AD). Although production and the economy in general registered little progress, many achievements were made in the realms of culture and science. The mathematician Zhu Chongzhi's calculation of π, the ratio of the circumference of a circle to its diameter, was accurate to seven decimal places. Other important scientific works of that time were *Commentary of the Waterways Classics* by the geographer Li Daoyuan, and *Important Arts for People's Welfare* by the agricultural scientist Jia Sixie.

In the realms of art and literature, the poems and prose of Zuo Si and the calligraphy of Wang Xizhi were innovative and imaginative. The musical work, *Guang Ling Verse*, by Ji Kang, has been passed down, and is still regarded as a model of the refined Chinese traditional music style. The painter, Gu Kaizhi, is even today praised for his works. The prose and poetry of Tao Yuanming are still recited and loved. Liu Xie wrote his masterpiece *Carving a Dragon at the Core of Literature* and Zhong Rong created his *Critique of Poetry*, the earliest systematic treatise on the "inherent law" of literature and poetry. Cao Cao and his sons, Cao Pi and Cao Zhi (jointly known as the Three Caos) are regarded as the ever-brightly shining stars of Chinese literature, with their masterpieces.

Buddhist relics include the Yungang Grottoes near Datong, Shanxi Province, and the Longmen Grottoes in Luoyang, Henan Province, both carved during the Northern Wei Dynasty (386-534 AD). Another grotto in Dunhuang, Gansu Province was created during the Sixteen States Period (304-439 AD).

The Wei, Jin and the Northern and Southern Dynasties together constituted a period of ethnic integration. In the north particularly, the assimilation of the Han and non-Han ethnic groups continued for almost 150 years. The merging of these ethnic groups was reflected in the cultural relics of the time (for example, the statues of Buddhas in grottoes). It is unquestionable that many Han surnames originated with non-Han people. This kind of open exchange greatly aided the development of Chinese civilization. It paved the way for prosperity during the blossoming of the Tang Dynasty, as well as aiding in unification.

The Sui and Tang Dynasties

The second peak of China's feudal society was the Sui and Tang period. This was the most brilliant and gorgeous age in the history of China.

In 581 AD, Yang Jian, a great general of the Northern Zhou Kingdom, forced the ruler to abdicate, and assumed power. He proclaimed himself Emperor

and began the Sui Dynasty. Chang'an was made his capital.
Having eliminated military threats posed by the northern
Turks, Yang Jian led his army into South China. At the
beginning of the year 589, it took only four months for
his army to defeat the Chen kingdom and to unite China.
Yang Jian, then known as Emperor Wen of Sui,
implemented a series of reforms. As a result, the Sui
Dynasty became wealthy and its people prospered. The
population grew and granaries swelled, inspiring the state
to issue a decree to "let the wealth and riches remain
with the people". The territory of China by then stretched
from the ocean in the east to the deserts in the west,
boasting a power and prosperity rarely seen in history.
However, the second son of Yang Jian murdered his
father and his elder brother, and ascended to the throne.
He was the notorious Emperor Yang of Sui, famous
even today for his debauchery and despotism. During
his reign, the powerful Sui Dynasty met its demise and
was finished. Only the Grand Canal, excavated in his
reign, is left as a positive accomplishment: the canal
is still functioning today.

Colorful dress of
the Tang Dynasty

The Tang Dynasty was established amidst wars and battles against the Sui,
acquiring by default the wealth and power of the short-lived Sui Dynasty. Among
the Tang emperors, there were two who stood out. One was Tang Taizong, or Li
Shimin, who took over the throne by murdering his elder brother and forcing the
abdication of his father in the Xuanwu Gate Coup d'État. Another was Tang
Xuanzong, or Li Longji (also known as Tang Minghuang). He was the grandson of
Wu Zetian, the only empress in the Chinese history. This Emperor and stories

A famous Chinese painting: "Ladies of the Kingdom of Guo on a spring excursion"

about him are still favorite subjects of contemporary literature, movies and television productions.

Tang Taizong (Li Shimin) had learned from the debilitating warfare and the ultimate demise of Sui Dynasty the lesson that "water can overturn the boat as well as keep it afloat." He instituted a policy of lowering taxation and corvées to avoid imposing too high a burden on farmers and craftsmen. He encouraged frugality and productivity. As a result, the economy boomed. Tang Taizong was also humble enough to encourage the free airing of views. He recruited the best and most virtuous people to fill offices and implement the civil administration examinations. In dealing with ethnic minorities, he substituted the encouragement of inter-marriage between the groups for conquering them by force. Peaceful and friendly exchanges were conducted between the Han people and other ethnic groups. During his reign, the period was known as the"peace and prosperity of Zheng Guan" (Zheng Guan being the imperial epithet of Tang Taizong).

The apogee of the Tang Dynasty appeared during the reign of Tang Xuanzong (712-756). The state was well organized, and people prospered. Tang Xuanzong was blessed with good fortune. His forefathers had laid a solid foundation for the Dynasty and his grandmother, Wu Zetian, had consolidated the central

authority and the royal family's reign. When he was young, Tang Xuanzong worked diligently to put both the civil administration and military forces in order. He employed the services of honest and virtuous men, and made the bureaucratic system more efficient. A peaceful political situation helped to insure social and economic development. Commerce boomed, boosted by a healthy agricultural sector. Taking advantage of the country's increased economic strength, Tang Xuanzong fortified the frontier defenses, and consolidated the northern borders. He insured the security of the Gansu and Hexi Corridors west of the Yellow River, a major link with Central Asia. The power and splendor of Chang'an, the capital of the Tang Dynasty, drew large numbers of foreign diplomats as well as merchants from European states and Asian countries. Tang Xuanzong inaugurated a nationwide census, and established a land-ownership register. These measures resulted in a rationalization of state finances, enhancing state revenues. With its position dominating the eastern part of Asia and as the leading civilization in Asia, the Tang Dynasty effectively assumed the role of center of the world in its time. Foreigners residing in Chang'an, including diplomatic corps, merchants and migrants, numbered more than thirty thousand. With pedestrians roaming the network of high streets, and commodities filling shelves in stores, song and dance being staged in theaters and hotels, Chang'an was then the most bustling, cosmopolitan area in the world. It is a pity that the city of Chang'an was later destroyed in the fires of war, and buried underneath dust and mud. What remains of the city of Chang'an was built in the Ming Dynasty. The surviving relics from the Tang Dynasty are just the Dayan Pagoda and the Blue Dragon Temple, which, standing alone under the sky, serve as a reminder of past glory.

The Tang Dynasty represented the splendor and brilliance of feudal China, and was the most open and advanced country in the world in its time. Both land and marine routes had been established between China and the rest of the world. Commerce extended to regions in the Pacific Ocean, and as far as the Mediterranean and Indian Oceans. East Asian and Persian merchants were seen all over China, buying and selling. Trade was active also between Tang and West Asia, and North Africa. Delegations from religious bodies, scholars and students traveled thousands of miles to visit China. Japan dispatched more than ten delegations to China to reside and study in Chang'an. Government officials, monks and craftsmen learned the trades of China. These visitors helped to spread the advanced cultures of the Tang Dynasty to many regions.

The Sui and Tang Dynasties led the world in science, literature, astronomy, medicine, philosophy, architecture, painting, music, dance and even in high fashion and social etiquette. Many of their arts and practices were learned, then imitated, by East Asian countries and survive until this day.

Xuanzuang traveled to India and brought back Buddhist scriptures to China. These scriptures were placed in storage in the Hong Fu Temple in Chang'an. Buddhism began to be introduced from India, and the center of the religion started to shift towards China. Christianity and Islam were introduced at about the same time. Cultures, customs and products from various foreign states were merging with those of China, and some were gradually assimilated. These were later regarded as "home-grown and native" to the land. They included fruit and musical instruments from Xinjiang and Central Asia, brocade from Persia, statues from India and medicinal books and herbs from Korea.

Literature in the Tang Dynasty was even more brilliant. Vibrant and active in literary circles in the early years of the Dynasty were the Four Outstanding Men of Letters — Wang Bo, Yang Jiong, Lu Zhaolin and Luo Binwang. In the heyday of the Tang Dynasty, there were the "Frontier School Poets" such as Gao Shi and Cen Cen. Others like Wang Wei and Meng Haoran, illustrious in describing natural beauty, were as respected as were the stars in the night sky. The best among the poets were the immortal poet Li Bai and the "poet among poets" Du Fu. Their works have become an integral part of Chinese culture. Followers such as Bai Juyi, Han Yu, Meng Jiao, Li He, Du Mu and Li Shangyin were all great poets, each with their own individual characteristics.

A peerless treasure: an agate cup in the shape of an animal's head, from the Tang Dynasty

In 1987, the underground cellar of Famen Temple in Fufeng, Xianyang City, Shaanxi, was excavated. Relics from the Tang Dynasty saw sunshine for the first time in over 800 years. Among them were Buddha's finger and various sacrificial articles including gold, silver, jade and colored glazed ware. Also found were top-grade greenish porcelain ware, which had been reserved for the Tang royal family: these were thought to have been lost forever. The magnificently decorated cellar of the Esoteric Mantra Sector was not only a place of enlightenment, with round and square altars on which Buddhas and Bodhisattvas were placed and sacrifices offered, but also serves as evidence that the center of Buddhism had shifted to China. The sacrificial articles reveal a clue to the wealth and a taste of the glory of the Tang Dynasty. Archeologists at the site did not have to work out the dates and origin of the articles, for there was already a detailed inventory of everything there. The names of the craftsmen were also carved in stone at the site and unearthed at the same time. These relics help to shed more light on the spread of Buddhism as well as the manner of religious conduct, and teaching. They also assist historians in learning more about tea, textiles, dyeing, the use of colored glaze, gold and silver-working, jade carving and Sino-foreign cultural exchange.

The cellar is itself a living library and museum. The relics represent the culture and craftsmanship of the Tang Dynasty during the period from the middle of the Dynasty to later years. Although the full glory and splendor of the flowering of Tang has disappeared forever, its signs are still breathtaking and impressive.

Chinese civilization ebbed after the golden ages of the Sui and Tang Dynasties. The 53 years after the dethronement of the last emperor of the Tang Dynasty was called the Five Dynasties and Ten States Period (907-979 AD). States and kingdoms were jousting during this period; conflicts and wars never ended. South China was relatively peaceful at this time, and agricultural production began to catch up with the north.

The Song and Yuan Dynasties

When Zhao Kuangyin established the Song Dynasty (960-1279 AD), he chose Bianjing (modern-day Kaifeng) as his capital. This period is generally known as the Northern Song Dynasty (960-1127 AD). The rulers were later forced to move to Lin'an (modern-day Hangzhou) and that became the capital of the Southern Song Dynasty (1127-1279 AD). The Song Dynasty endured for 320 years and saw the reign of 18 emperors. However, both the Northern and Southern

Song Dynasties were militarily weak. The strength of the state was in decline and its territory kept on shrinking. Although Zhao Kuangyin was regarded as an enlightened emperor, he could not resolve the conflicts with the powerful northern nomads. The Song Dynasty continually engaged itself in war with the states of the northern ethnic minorities, such as the Liao, the Jin and the Xixia. Over more than three centuries, the rulers of the Song Dynasty always ruled with their hearts in the mouths.

Despite this, the Song Dynasty played an essential role in the evolution of Chinese culture. It was an age in which philosophy, religion and various schools of thought merged with and differentiated from one another. These ideas and thoughts were compared, debated, reorganized and summarized, causing their frameworks to take shape. Li Xue, the Confucian school of idealist philosophy, became prominent and dominated mainstream ideology. Scholars annotated and expounded on the mainstream Confucian classics. Chinese philosophy crystallized, embodying Confucianism, Buddhism and Taoism. It had a tight theoretical structure and at the same time openly embraced the essence of foreign cultures and ideas, serving as the root of Chinese civilization, and yet leaving room for future development. Despite its weakness, the Song Dynasty's cultural accomplishments earn it a unique position in Chinese history.

The Northern Song Dynasty boasted a relatively complete civil administration system. It served as a precursor of the civil service system in quite a few countries.

The early years of the Northern Song Dynasty were indeed days of prosperity. A painted scroll entitled "Life along the River during the Qingming Festival", by Zhang Zeduan, depicts a bustling scene in the capital. Boats go up and down the river, products and produce pile as high as small hills. Shops extend in long lines, and carts and pedestrians crowd the streets. Unfortunately, this peace and prosperity did not last long. While the lanterns and lamps were lit in the imperial capital, beacon-fires were also relaying signals on the frontier. The Dynasty found it hard

**Part of the painting
"Life along the River
during the Qingming
Festival"**

to defend itself when two of their emperors, Song Huizong and Song Qinzong
were abducted by Jin invaders. Authorities were forced to give up the northern
capital and moved to the south and the emperors and their courts, were too weak
and timid to assert their rule.

While the Southern Song Dynasty and the Jin faced each other in a stalemate,
the northern Mongol nomadic tribes led by Timujin (1167-1227) came to the
fore. He unified the Mongols and proclaimed himself Genghis Khan. He, his sons
and grandsons led the great Mongol army westward. In half a century, Mongol
horsemen staged three large-scale incursions into Europe. The conquests of
Genghis Khan established empires in what is today Xinjiang, Russia, Iran and
Central Asia. After more than 40 years of resisting the Mongols, the Southern
Song Dynasty at last met its end, defeated by the Mongol warriors. In 1271 AD,
Kublai Khan established his empire, Da Yuan, in central China and based his
court in today's Beijing; he named it "Da Du", or "the Great Capital". The Yuan
Dynasty became the first in China's history to establish nationwide rule by a
single ethnic minority.

The first achievement of the Yuan Dynasty was ending the disunity and
fractionalization of China that characterized the 370 years after the Tang Dynasty.
Continuous wars and fighting were put to an end, and the country was unified

once again with different ethnic groups living side-by-side. The territory of the Yuan Dynasty extended even further than that of the Tang Dynasty, giving shape to the territory of modern China.

The central authorities of the Yuan Dynasty set up in the capital an organization overseeing both the administrative and religious affairs of Tibet. During the Dynasty, Tibet had become a formal administrative region. The various minorities in Yun'nan, southwestern China, also came under the direct control of the central authorities. Penghu Policing Forces were also put in place to take charge of islands such as Penghu and Liuqiu. Taiwan was included in the territory of the Yuan Dynasty.

Sino-foreign exchanges had reached a high point in the history of China by then. Trade links were established with countries in Europe, Asia and Africa. An Italian, Marco Polo, lived for 17 years in the territories of the Yuan Dynasty when the empire was in its prime. Upon returning to his home country, he wrote *The Travels of Marco Polo*. Although there were inaccuracies in his descriptions, his accounts inspired long and undying curiosity about - and longing for - China.

The authorities of the Yuan Dynasty adopted an open policy toward religious issues. All religions flourished, notably Islam. A new ethnic group, Hui, who worshiped Islam but spoke Chinese, began to take form during the Yuan and later, the Ming Dynasties.

Starting from the mid-Yuan Dynasty, politics became more and more murky. Ethnic suppression and class conflicts intensified and multiplied. This resulted in simultaneous uprisings in many places. In 1368, troops led by Zhu Yuanzhang overran and conquered Da Du. That victory dealt the final blow to the dying Dynasty. The Yuan regime had lasted for 98 years, starting from Kublai Khan's enthronement to its end.

During the Song and Yuan period, beyond cultural achievements, accomplishments in science and technology were also impressive. Ancient China's four great inventions, the compass, gunpowder, papermaking and printing, all became widely utilized. Moveable-type printing was developed. The compass was used in marine navigation, enabling China to sail what was then the world's largest fleet. Munitions factories produced rockets similar to the ordnance of today. The world's earliest cannon with a cylinder-shaped barrel was first used in the Yuan Dynasty. Shen Kuo, a great scientist of the Song Dynasty, wrote his masterpiece on science and technology, *Sketchbook of Dream Brook*. Guo Shoujing, an astronomer in the Yuan Dynasty, led the construction of the finest observatory in the capital Da Du. Huang Daopo, a woman textile expert, made innovations in spinning and weaving machinery, giving great impetus to the textile industry of that time.

In the field of literature, Su Dongpo, Li Qingzhao, Xin Qiji and Lu You were all great poets of the Song Dynasty. Their works are favorites of many even today, and will surely continue to capture the imaginations of generations to come. Dramatists such as Guan Hanqing, Wang Shipu, Bai Pu and Ma Zhiyuan raised the Chinese art of drama to a higher level of maturity.

Studies and research by the Cheng Hao and Cheng Yi brothers as well as Zhu Xi recapitulated and summarized traditional Chinese philosophic thought and presented a unified theoretic framework. *Historical Events Retold as a Mirror of Government*, the first general history of China, compiled by Sima Guang, gave an account of more than 1,300 years of history. Representing a milestone in the chronological approach to the compilation of history, the book serves as a reminder to learn from the lessons of the past.

Of course, one cannot ignore Premier Wang Anshi's reforms during the Northern Song Dynasty. He strove to solve the conflict of interest between the landowners and their tenant farmers in order to strengthen the feudal establishment. Wang also sought to "enrich both the masses and the state" with a stronger and more efficient central finance system. Unfortunately, in spite of his good intentions and best efforts, his reforms failed.

All these lessons and achievements paved the way for later developments in the Ming and Qing Dynasties.

The Ming and Qing Dynasties

The Ming Dynasty began in 1368 AD, locating its administrative center in Ying Tian Fu (modern-day Nanjing.) In the early years of the Dynasty, China still led the world in development and the economy continued to progress. The region south of the Yangtze River, which became the economic center during the Five Dynasties and Ten States Period, also led the way in moving towards a civil society during the Ming Dynasty. Local commerce and external trade were active there. Zhu Yuanzhang, the founder of the Ming Dynasty, adopted a series of policies that were aimed at rejuvenating production, and returning the people to their normal lives. The new empire soon stood on its own feet. After Zhu Yuanzhang's death, Zhu Di won the contest for the throne and assumed the title of Emperor. He was Ming Chengzhu, also known as Emperor Yong Le.

Ming Chengzhu undertook three major tasks during his reign:

First, he moved the capital to Beijing. In the 19th year of Zhu Di's reign (1421), the move to Beijing was finally accomplished. The present layout of the city follows that of the Beijing of that time.

Second, he dispatched Zheng He (1371-1435) on voyages to the Western Seas (i.e. seas and lands west of the South China Sea). Zhu Di also decreed that "forces must not be dispatched to conquer the fifteen states in South China Sea" i.e., there must be a peaceful diplomatic approach. The most powerful and technologically advanced fleets were assembled and embarked on seven voyages to spread the glory and culture of China, in addition to carrying out commerce.

Third, he authorized the compilation of *Yong Le Da Dian*, or *Great Encyclopedia of Yong Le*. It was the earliest and biggest encyclopedia of its time in China and in the world. Altogether 22,877 volumes comprised the work. Unfortunately, only about 800 volumes are left today; the rest were destroyed in later years, especially during the invasion by the Western powers into Beijing in 1900. The volumes were either burned or smuggled out of China.

From the mid-Ming Dynasty China's economy was free to flourish. Townships and villages shot up in southeast China, boasting new kinds of handicrafts and commercial activities. Some farmers abandoned the land and became merchants and traders, and others, without any capital, became craftsmen. They constituted the new civil society of China, concentrating in towns and cities. The rise of these classes with their entrepreneurship as well as their free-thinking and liberal styles were portrayed vividly in novels and storytellers' scripts during the Ming and Qing Dynasties. The practice of "rent in kind", that had been practiced for more than a thousand years, began to be replaced by monetary rent in the more commercially developed regions. Silver, as legal tender, became widely accepted. Although paper currency as legal tender appeared during the Song Dynasty, it gained popularity in the Ming Dynasty. More and more silk, porcelain, tea, and gunny and cotton cloth were exported in return for silver. The populations of Nanjing and Beijing each grew to over one million. Thousands of boats swarmed on the Grand Canal, their canvasses flying in the wind, displaying a breath-taking scene. Wu Chang and Han Yang, both located on the Yangtze River, turned into commerce centers.

However, troubles were brewing, from both internal and external sources. Pirates from Holland, Spain and Portugal were attacking seaside villages. Japanese pirates, and unscrupulous Chinese coastal traders and merchants, harassed seaside dwellers. Inland, homeless people migrated from one place to another. In the court, power was wielded by eunuchs, and injustice was

The design drawing of the Forbidden City in Beijing

rampant. The Nü Zhen tribe in northeastern Liaoning was catching up in strength and power and posed an increasingly grave threat to the Ming regime.

In 1644, Li Zicheng led his followers in a peasant uprising. His army succeeded in one battle after another, and they finally broke into the capital city of Beijing. Emperor Chongzhen, the last ruler of Ming, hanged himself on Mount Mei in Beijing. His death marked the end of the Ming Dynasty, which had endured for 277 years. However, Li failed to establish his own regime. A Manchu emperor who came to throne and ended the Ming Dynasty.

Upon the entry of their great armies into northern China, the Manchu authorities tried at first to exercise a strategy of clearing large areas. However,

The court robe worn by Emperor Tongzhi when he was enthroned

they soon realized that driving the people off their land and letting the troops move in simply did not work. Wherever the Manchu warriors went, the Han majority people greatly resented their presence. Disputes arose over the hairstyle for men imposed by the Manchu authorities. This looked like a minor issue, but in fact it was representative of a principle — whether the Han subjects were entitled to preserve their own ethnic customs, or had to abandon them in order to get along with their Manchu rulers. It was also a debate as to whether the more advanced Han culture, traditions and practices should be followed, or the relatively backward production processes of the Manchus should be adopted nationwide. This conflict was clearly defined by the fact that the more advanced the local economy, the greater the protest and resistance to the Manchu orders and decrees. The people of southeastern China had long been regarded as the most civil and reserved people in the country. When it came to the fight to protect their own life styles, however, they proved to be even more unyielding and perseverant than their northern counterparts, who were generally thought to be more coarse and courageous.

As the Manchu forces laid siege to Yangzhou, just north of the downstream stretch of the Yangtze River, the people in the city staged a brave and heroic protest. When the defense of the town was finally broken, the Manchu went on a rampage of arson and massacre for ten days to avenge the efforts that they had exerted in the conquest. Another city, Jiading, put up a similarly brave resistance, and met with massacre thrice in the hands of the Manchu conquerors. The people of Jiangyin, a town on the south bank of the lower extremity of the Yangtze River, held out for more than 80 days. When the town was finally conquered, only 53 people were found alive. These recorded events serve as proof that the more economically developed regions resisted being taken over by a relatively less-developed economic system as well as the authorities that represented it.

The first several emperors of the Qing Dynasty, however, adopted a receptive attitude toward cultural issues. They were able to see beyond their own ethnic boundaries, and encouraged the absorption of advanced techniques and knowledge from various ethnic groups, inspired by the concept of all Chinese as being included in one nation. A political guideline for assimilation was implemented by the early rulers of the Qing Dynasty. For instance, western missionaries, such as Germany's Johann Adam Schall von Bell, were appointed as government officials in the Dynasty. The knowledge of physics, astronomy, mathematics and chemistry brought by the missionaries were eagerly received, and applied by the Chinese court. The reigns of Emperors Kangxi, Yongzheng and Qionglong were regarded as periods of peace and prosperity, as one of bright spots of feudal China. The outside world, in the meantime, was in the early stages of industrialization. The newly-emerged capital-based means of production served to release massive productivity. New machinery and factories were appearing one after another. The western world, which had lagged behind China in social and economic development, soon overtook and raced ahead. However, progress was still evident during the Ming and Qing Dynasties in China, especially during the early years of Qing. The early Manchu rulers were farsighted enough to implement a series of policies that bolstered social and economic rejuvenation. Unrest was dealt with and pacified, external threats were contained, and the territory of the Dynasty was maintained. A peaceful and steady political environment helped to nurture the economy. So, even though China lagged in technology and production methods, the aggregate strength of the country was still impressive when compared to other nations. Starting with a population of no more than 100 million in the early days of Qing, China grew to 400 million by the end of the Dynasty. This population growth alone was a good indicator of the sustainability of China's economy.

What was needed for this ancient civilization, arriving at the crossroads of its history, was innovation and adaptation. The feudal rulers, however, maintained a tight grip on ideology, thought and culture. New sprouts, as fast as they appeared, were rooted out. A nation-wide closed-door policy imposed by the authorities served as a barrier, preventing communication with the outside world. China's development lagged and slowed, while its western peers continued to move forward; the West caught up and left China behind in economic strength, technology and military power.

The Opium War, which broke out in 1840, changed the course of the history of the country. China gradually slipped into a semi-colonial state and a nearly-subjugated society.

However, the Chinese people are not without their brave heroes. Many courageous men and women of the country came to the fore, and devoted their wisdom and energy to the cause of China's renaissance.

On September 20, 1838, Lin Zexu submitted a report to Emperor Daoguang recommending the curtailment of the spread of opium addiction. His suggestion was accepted, and he was dispatched to Guangdong to oversee the issue acting as the Emperor's commissioner. Lin acted quickly and decisively in Gaungdong: he

burned large consignments of
opium that had been confiscated at
Humen. Undeterred by the more
advanced gunboats and more
powerful cannons of the British
expedition, Lin led both soldiers and
civilians in Guangzhou in battling the armed

A treasure of
Empress
Dowager Cixi

opium traffickers. The weak and timid central authorities of the Qing Dynasty, however,
acceded to the immediate pressure of the British navy. In the end, as a result of
Sino-British negotiations, Lin was banished, and the Nanjing Protocol, the first unequal
treaty conceding rights to foreign invaders, was signed. In the summer of 1842, Lin
went into exile to Ili, Xinjiang, a barren land in western-most China.

One of Lin Zexu's closest associates was Wei Yuan. Lin Zexu had once presided
over the compilation of *A Record of the Nations of the World*. Wei Yuan took
over the project, and expanded its contents. In 1842, a fifty-volume *Maps and
Records of the Nations of the World* was accomplished. The work was later
expanded to 60 volumes, and then to 100 volumes by 1852. It was the definitive
work of its time, with research and writing wholly undertaken by Chinese scholars.
It presented a milestone in China's efforts to understand the outside world. The
book unveiled to Chinese readers the real circumstances in the world at that
time, playing a great role in their enlightenment. It also produced a positive
impact on Japan's Meiji Reformation (1868-1912).

On January 11, 1851, Hong Xiuquan initiated the Taiping Heavenly Kingdom
Revolution, a peasant uprising in its most modern sense. Two years later, on
March 19, 1853, Hong Xiuquan and his men conquered Nanjing. Hong renamed
the city Tianjing and made it the capital of his regime. The System of Land
Ownership of the Heavenly Kingdom was promulgated. Equality between men
and women was advocated. A locally administered system for the defense of the

land was instituted to resist foreign incursions. However, Hong Xiuquan and his regime were aloof and out of touch with the people. Infighting at the top was rampant, and weakened the regime. The regime's enemies, domestic and external, took advantage of the internal disunity and dealt the final blow to the revolution. In 1864, the capital Tianjing was put under siege. Hong Xiuquan died of illness on June 1, the eve of the fall of the city. The end of the uprising came on July 19 of that year, when the capital was finally taken.

The Qing rulers became increasingly weak in the later years of the Dynasty. Under the repeated incursions by the western powers and their incessant demands for concessions, the Qing Dynasty had to cede territory and pay indemnities to make peace. Now, China faced the fate of being divided up piecemeal. Some of the more enlightened intellectuals started to seek the best way out for the country, under the real threat of being vanquished. They saw that countries such as Russia and Japan had managed to rise to power through reform, and thought that China could do the same. Led by Kang Youwei, the reformists plotted to stage a reform movement aimed at adopting a new legal system and pursuing economic growth and strength.

Born in 1858 in Nanhai, Kang Youwei was a native of Guangdong. Liang Qichao, fifteen years younger and a native of Xinhui County, Gaungdong, was his student. They were both leaders of the reformist party. In June 1894, both went to the capital Beijing to undertake the national-level imperial examinations. The next month, Japan initiated the Sino-Japanese War of 1894-1895. On April 15, 1895, the Qing government was forced to sign, in the capacity of the defeated party, the Sino-Japanese Treaty of Shimonoseki. This was a great humiliation for China. More than a thousand imperial examination candidates in Beijing from 18 Provinces were indignant at the news. The candidates from Taiwan were particularly infuriated over the provision in the treaty that ceded Taiwan to Japan. They submitted a petition to the top authorities that was "written and presented over tears". As arranged by Kang Youwei, Liang Qichao undertook the task of liaison and networking. On May 1, 1895, over 1300 candidates from all 18 Provinces gathered in the Song Yun Convent (today's Da Zhi Bridge outside Xuan Wu Gate, Beijing). Kang Youwei made an emotional speech at the meeting, describing the humiliation suffered by China under the Sino-Japanese Treaty of Shimonoseki. Kang expounded on his idea that the country could not expect to be spared an ill fate unless reforms were implemented. Indignation resounded among the candidates. They elected Kang as their spokesman to deliver a petition to Emperor Guangxu. Kang drafted a petition of more than 10,000 words and submitted it to the Emperor. The petition advanced suggestions for the Emperor "to issue decrees to boost the morale of the people"; "to train the military forces to stand up to outside threats"; and to "implement reforms to seek more stable and enlightened policies". The petition was submitted to the court on May 2nd. This was the famous "Plea by the National Imperial Examination Candidates". Although the petition failed to reach Emperor Guangxu, it represented a courageous and patriotic deed on the part of Kang and his followers. Kang passed the national examination. He then submitted another plea to the Emperor, at the end of May. This time, the Emperor read it and was pleased. Kang Youwei and Liang Qichao felt that there was a need to promote the idea of reform. They organized an association and gathered around them a group of men who shared similar ideals and visions. Kang also funded *A Gazette of the Nations of the World*, later renamed *Journal of Home and Abroad.* The publication, in newspaper form, was distributed together with the *Capital News* (the capital's official newspaper). In 1897, German forces entered and occupied Jiaozhou Bay in Shandong and the Russians forced their way into Lü Shun Kou and Dalian Bay. Once again China faced the threat of being dismembered. Kang and Liang saw this as another opportunity to make a new petition. They traveled north to Beijing and submitted another plea to Emperor Guangxu. Although it failed again to reach the desk of the Emperor under constraints imposed by the conservatives, the petition was circulated among officials in the capital. Newspapers in Tianjin and Shanghai also carried the message. On the morning of January 24, 1898, Emperor Guangxu summoned Kang Youwei for an audience at the General Administrator's office. On January 29, for the sixth time, Kang filed a plea to the Emperor. The young Emperor was impressed with Kang's proposal and read his petition numerous times. On June 11, Emperor Guangxu issued a series of "decrees of reforms concerning state affairs", tossing out the old educational system and retiring redundant officials. New institutions and practices were encouraged, such as modern schools, newspapers, other avenues for people to express their opinions, and the employment of reformists in the advocacy and implementation of new measures. These reforms were promoted for 103 days and ended on September 21, 1898. This was known in China's history as "The Hundred Days Reform". The conservatives, led by Empress Dowager Cixi, mounted a coup in the court and confined Emperor Gaungxu in Yingtai in the Forbidden City. Kang Youwei and Liang Qichao took refuge in Japan. At four o'clock in the afternoon on September 28, 1898, six of the reformists were executed at Caishi Kou, a crossroad in the center of Beijing. Upon arriving in Japan, Kang Youwei and Liang Qichao continued to promote reforms to save the country from its plight. Academically, both of them had also made notable achievements, especially Liang Qichao.

The Revolution of 1911

As history turned over a new leaf in the 20th century, great changes took place in China. On October 10, 1911, the revolutionary Dr. Sun Yat-sen led the Wuchang Uprising, leading to the downfall of the Qing Dynasty. In the following year, the Republic of China was established.

Sun Yat-sen (1866-1925), also known as Sun Zhongshan and Sun Wen, was born in Cuiheng Village, Xiangshan County, Guangdong. He later went to Honolulu with his mother, and studied at Iolani School and Oahu School, both run by westerners. It was during that time that Sun Yat-sen came into contact with western social and political theories, and natural sciences. In 1883, he enrolled in the Diocesan Boy's School in Hong Kong. The next year, he transferred to Yuduoli College, and then to the Nanhua Medical School, before being enrolled in the Hong Kong College of Medicine for Chinese. At first, Dr. Sun Yat-sen wished to engage the world in the capacity of a doctor. He later realized that "medicine saves few and little", and gave up his profession in favor of politics. In the winter of 1894 in Honolulu, he organized the first democratic revolutionary body for China, the Xing Zhong Hui, or the China Renaissance Society. The next year, collaborating with Chen Shaobaï, Zhen Shiliang and others, he staged the First Guangzhou Armed Uprising. He took refuge in Japan when the uprising failed, and he was sought by the Qing authorities. He went on to New York and then to London, where he was kidnapped by agents dispatched by the Qing Dynasty's embassy in London. Under pressure from his friends and acquaintances in China and abroad, the Qing authorities finally released him. When the Boxer Uprising started in 1900, Dr. Sun simultaneously initiated an uprising in Huizhou. Though it ended in failure, it won widespread recognition from the grassroots and intellectuals. On August 20, 1905, Dr. Sun allied with other revolutionary organizations in Japan and created the Chinese Revolutionary League. Dr. Sun served as the premier, and he also started the party newspaper-*Ming Bao*. In his introduction to the newspaper, Dr. Sun Yat-sen first put forward the Three Principles of the People, which were "Nationalism, Democracy and the

People's Livelihood". In October 1911, the Wuchang Uprising succeeded. In December, Dr. Sun was appointed as the ad hoc president of the Republic of China. Then, Yuan Shikai, engaging in some Machiavellian maneuvers, tricked the revolutionaries and grabbed the temporary presidency. Even before Yuan Shikai murdered his comrade revolutionaries, Dr. Sun realized his grave mistake in recommending Yuan Shikai as his successor and issued the "Decree of Fighting against Yuan Shikai", starting the "Second Revolution". Unfortunately, this revolution also ended in failure. Dr. Sun once again fled to Japan to reorganize the Chinese revolutionary party in order to return to China to fight against Yuan Shikai and defend the law. However, warlords in the north and the south conspired to force Dr. Sun out of the position of Grand Marshal of the army and navy. Under a "stay at home" order, he was forced to resign and went to Shanghai. Sun Yat-sen was very depressed. Fortunately, Lenin sent a representative to Dr. Sun to discuss conditions in the Far East and to offer assistance to the Chinese revolutionary cause; this was heartening news to Dr. Sun. On August 23, 1922, a representative of the CPC, Li Dazhao, met Sun Yat-sen in Shanghai, and they reached agreement on cooperation between the two parties. On September 4, 1922, Sun Yat-sen convened a meeting to reorganize the KMT. In November 1923, he issued the declaration giving the terms of the party's reorganization, restated the "Three Principles of the People", and reaffirmed the three-point policy of "Ally with Russia, Ally with the CPC and Help the Farmer and the Worker". On January 20, 1924, the first National People's Congress of the KMT was held in Guangzhou; many CPC notables like Li Dazhao and Mao Zedong participated and were elected to either the central committee, or to the backup central committee of the KMT. In 1924, Dr. Sun Yat-sen suppressed the activities of the Guangdong business blocs. On November 13 of the same year, Dr. Sun and Song Qingling, traveled by ship to discuss state affairs with the Beijing government, then controlled by

Feng Yuxiang. As the ship passed Tianjin, Dr. Sun fell ill, but he insisted on continuing to Beijing to complete his mission. On May 12, 1925, at the age of sixty, this great revolutionary who had fought his whole life for democracy and the independence and the freedom of his country, drew his last breath.

The great significance of the Revolution of 1911 was that it ended the 2000 years of feudal and autocratic rule that had started in 221 BC. The Revolution once and for all put an end to the reign of emperors on the Chinese continent.

The May 4th Movement

Though the Revolution of 1911 created the Republic of China and abolished the emperor, a semi-colonial and semi-feudal social state still existed, and the corrupt culture of old still held sway over the people's lives.

After World War I, the treatment dealt to China by the Paris Peace Conference instigated a huge demonstration by Beijing students on May 4th, 1919. Students, workers and merchants all over China followed suit; on June 3rd, workers in Shanghai went on strike, and then workers in major cities all over the country followed. Classes were suspended, and businesses were closed. This fiery grassroots rebellion was known as the May 4th Movement.

The May 4th Movement put forward the slogans "Put an End to Confucianism" and "Up With Democracy and Science". It further advocated the introduction of new thought, new ideas and new methods, which China then lacked, using "Democracy and Science" as their banner and battle cry.

The Movement, which swept out the undesirable elements of the known and welcomed the new, was of profound significance. Many western concepts, which had previously been barred, now flowed into China like a river, and opened the minds of vast number of Chinese intellectuals whose access to outside sources of knowledge had long been blocked. The Movement let the Chinese people view the broad sky through a widening crack; lungs that had been constricted for so long were now able to breathe freely the air of new cultures to their heart's content. The so-called "new culture" on the one hand meant a wide range of disciplines: philosophy, science, literature, arts, aesthetics and the economics of capitalism; on the other hand, it meant the new ideology of the proletariat, Marxism and Leninism. After the opening of the gate, novel ideas gushed into the country; all of them were seen as "new minds, new cultures".

The most direct effect of May 4th Movement was the birth of the Communist Party of China. In July, 1921, twelve representatives gathered in Shanghai and held the First Congress of the CPC. The party, which at that time had only a few dozens of members, put forward the slogan "Overthrow the Old China". The world barely took notice of this event, but in later years it became apparent that history had given to the CPC the task of entombing the Old China.

On October 1st, 1949, Mao Zedong announced with a tremulous voice from the gate of the Tian'anmen Square of Beijing to the whole world: "The People's Government of the People's Republic of China is founded today!" It was then that the whole world realized that this momentous change had begun on that hot day in July, 1921.

During the past century, China experienced three great transformations: the first was the Revolution of 1911, which overthrew the feudal monarchy which had lasted thousands of years; the second was the founding of the People's Republic of China, which transformed China into a socialist country;

the third was the Opening and Reform, during which China entered the period of socialist modernization. Three great figures were behind these changes: Sun Yat-Sen, Mao Zedong and Deng Xiaoping. Their unrelenting spirit and distinguished achievements in leading the Chinese people searching for the road to strength and prosperity will go down in history forever.

Some Characteristics of Chinese History

The nation of China developed, one step after another, in a long-flowing succession of eras. Looking back on its history, one can discern several distinct characteristics, which are worthy of remembering.

First, the Chinese civilization is the only civilization in the world that has an unbroken history of development. It is ancient, and it is also modern. Its qualities underpin its vitality now, and in the future.

Ancient human civilizations were precursors of today's civilizations, but the ancient civilizations of Mesopotamia, Egypt or India were all afflicted and disrupted by wars, and finally exterminated by the invasion of foreign nations. The rupture of these civilizations is one of the tragedies of human existence, and is an inevitable misfortune. It was precisely because of its own power that Chinese civilization was able to withstand the assaults and invasions by so many foreign elements even with their gunships and airplanes. China steadfastly held its position, in the process of defending itself and absorbing the benefits of foreign civilizations to enrich the country.

Second, the history of China is a history of constant internal merging and fusing. Every member of the Chinese nation, of whatever ethnicity, has made his own contribution to the whole of the Chinese civilization.

During the country's long history, there were several important phases of internal adjustments to accommodate the various ethnic groups. This bringing-together was an endless process and a good example of cross-fertilization and assimilation. It was this open and harmonious characteristic of the Chinese nation that ensured its continuous regeneration and development. China showed the same openness to foreign influences: Buddhism originated in India, but the center of the religion finally became lodged in China, and Buddhist thought became one of the three pillars of Chinese traditional culture. This is a vivid example of China's willingness and ability to absorb the merits of other cultures to its own benefit and use - this is why Chinese civilization extended for thousands of years of unbroken history.

Third, in Chinese history, the central government, presiding over the unification of many ethnic groups, was the main force of the nation.

Since the Qin and Han Dynasties, unity was the mainstream, and separation was the tributaries. A unified country encompassing many ethnic groups was the

The Imperial Palace
in Beijing

basic and stable base of the Chinese state's regime. After the first emperor of Qin united China, the Chinese were united for far longer periods than they were separated. Even during the periods of separation, China never stopped the process of merging and assimilating. So for most of the country's history, all ethnic groups lived together in a unified country.

Fourth, though China's history is replete with accounts of war, turmoil, barbarism and cruelty, it never resorted to wars, oppression or force when dealing with the outside world. The external advances of the Chinese nation were carried out by peaceful means.

Fifth, the reason that the Chinese nation has a sturdy, cohesive constitution is because it has an enviable cultural tradition which is embraced by the whole nation. Solid values and moral standards are the spiritual Great Wall of the nation, accumulated, tested and refined during centuries of practice. Possessing these outstanding values and morals is one of the reasons why the Chinese nation has never been conquered or assimilated by another.

Chinese Characters, a Script Both Ancient and Modern

Chapter Four

Exactly when language first came into use is still a mystery. Language distinguishes human beings from animals.

The birth of written characters was another great leap forward: this development enabled humans to name and explain things, to capture and pass down human feelings and thoughts. The history of a nation's written characters is a monument to its cultural heritage.

Block characters are the very symbols — and records — of Chinese civilization.

—

A History of Square-Shaped Chinese Characters

Oracle bone inscriptions had characters used in the Shang Dynasty, more than 3000 years ago, and using a systematic set of written symbols.

Left: A tortoise shell

Approximately 5000 inscription characters have been discovered, and about 2000 of them have been deciphered. The characters have been placed in categories such associative compounds, hieroglyphs, phonetic loan words and others. They represent parts of speech as nouns, pronouns, verbs, adjectives, and numerals. The structure and word sequence of sentences were much the same as those of later ages. In the oracle bone inscriptions, there are such sentences as "it would be safe and free of trouble to travel both ways," "it does not rain today," "there is gusting wind today," and so on. These sentences are virtually the same as those used by the Chinese today, and serve as proof that before the oracle bones were inscribed, the written Chinese language must have had evolved for a long time. The discovery of carved marks on artifacts unearthed in Jiahu, Wuyang County, Henan Province in 1983 — these marks date back about more than 7000 years — indicates that Chinese characters might have been taking form more than 6000 years ago.

There are six ancient categories of Chinese characters, sorted according to the way they were created: pictographic characters, self-explanatory characters, combined-meaning characters, characters adopted to represent homophones,

This bell remains an enigma to us

mutually explanatory characters and pictophonetic characters. Examining these ancient characters helps explain the development of modern Chinese characters.

In a pictographic character or pictograph, a picture was drawn of the thing the character stood for, and the picture became the word. For instance, the sun was

Comparison of Ancient styles of Calligraphy

	small seal script	Western Zhou Dynasty (1100BC-771BC)	Warring States Period (475BC-221BC)					
			Qin	Chu	Qi	Yan	Three Jins	Zhongshan
马								
者								
市								
年								

written as ☉ or ⊖, the moon as ☽ or ☾. Numbers such as one, two, three and four were drawn as 一, 二, 三, 亖 respectively. Self-explanatory symbols, such as ● or ▬, were sometimes added to pictographs to form new characters. For instance, the edge of a knife was written as 刀, roots of a plant as 木, the end of a tree branch as 末, the color red as 朱, the word "inch" as 寸, and the word "also" or "too" as 亦.

Self-explanatory characters such as 上 ("above"), 下 ("below") are said to be the most primitive of Chinese characters. Self-explanatory characters make up the smallest category of characters in Chinese. In *Origin of the Chinese Characters*, an early Chinese dictionary, there were only 129 words that belong to this category.

A combined-meaning character is formed by putting together existing, related characters. For instance, the character 信("faith") is a combination of 人("person") and 言 ("word"), and means "keeping one's word".

There are characters adopted to represent homophones. In early times, frequently there was no written word to represent the spoken word. To solve the problem, a word with the same or similar pronunciation was borrowed to denote it. Linguists of the past noted this, and described the word invention in this way: "There is not such a word existing at all and a word of the same sound is borrowed to substitute it." The character 求(qiu), meaning "beg or petition" is a good example. The small seal script of the character is 求, which is a hieroglyph originally meaning "fur" or "hide". It happens to share the same pronunciation with the word "beg". This character was borrowed, and it took on new meanings in such compounds as "to ask for", "to demand", or "to pursue". These words are so popularly used today that the original meaning of the word, "fur" or "hide" has been forgotten. A new word, 裘, had to be created to mean specifically "fur" or "hide".

A mutually explanatory character is created by adding a radical to an existing character. The radical denotes a meaning and usually defines the category of the word. For instance, the Chinese word "snake" was written as 它 in the small seal script, and later evolved to 它. The simplified form of the word lost its hieroglyphic feature, as was its ability to represent the animal it originally denoted. Thus the radical 虫 ("animal") was added to link it to its original meaning.

A pictophonetic character is made up of two elements. One indicates the category of the meaning of the character, and the other the sound — the same or similar pronunciation to give the word its phonetic feature. The characters 江 and 河, meaning "big river" and "river" respectively, are good examples. They share the same component "氵", which stands for "water". The other half 工 or 可, denotes the sound of the word. There are many such words, for example: 铜 ("copper"), 烤 ("roast"), 领 ("collar"), 箭 ("arrow"), 煮 ("boil"), 闻 ("hear"), 园 ("garden"), 岛 ("island"), and 房 ("house").

Chinese characters have evolved from their primitive forms to their modern styles through many phases. The major styles include oracle bone inscriptions, bronze inscriptions during the Western and Eastern Zhou, scripts popular during the Warring States Period, and the seal script characteristic of the Qin Dynasty. These are the archaic forms and styles. Modern styles include the official script, regular script, cursive script and running script. Bronze inscriptions were those marked on bronze objects. Large and small seal scripts are characteristic of the Spring and Autumn and Warring States Period. After the Qin Dynasty had unified China, the chancellor, Li Si, sorted out the various scripts, and designated the small seal scripts as the standard written script. History has called this the "unification of characters". Regular script appeared later and came to be the popular and standard style of the Chinese written language, and is the one still in use today. As for the running and cursive scripts, both were created for efficiency in writing and as a form of art; they are supplemental to the regular script. Chinese characters have undergone processes of both complication and simplification during their evolution. Changes were effected in such aspects as the creation of new words, morphology, structure, the number of words, pronunciation, and connotation. Today, the language has developed to such a stage that both its linguistic efficiency and convenience for study and application have reached a historically high level. The Chinese people have always sought to perfect their language system, and the square-shaped characters are the result of their collective efforts.

=

Merits of
Chinese Characters and
Their Historic Contributions

The world's most ancient characters are all hieroglyphs, of three known types: the first are the cuneiforms created by the Sumerians on the Mesopotamia Plain; they appeared at approximately 3,000 BC. The second are the hieroglyphics of ancient Egypt — they had become mature by 3,000 BC. The third are the square-shaped Chinese characters, which appeared approximately 3,000 years ago.

Of all three types of characters, only the Chinese characters remain in use. The other two were lost over time as they fell into disuse, and now they are understood only by few scholars. Why, under the impact of so many changes in Chinese culture and the impact of foreign ones, could only Chinese characters keep developing? What is the source of their long-lasting sturdiness and vitality? Of all the main written languages of the human race, the Chinese characters are the only ancient ones still actively used in modern times.

First, Chinese characters are the only characters that have been able to transcend time and individual dialects.

Alphabetic languages currently have the leading role on the stage of world language and characters. The European languages are good examples. After the fall and disintegration of the ancient Roman Empire, the old Latin language gradually followed suit, and people in every part of Europe started to form their own dialects using the Roman alphabet. Then the Italian, French, Spanish, Portuguese and Romanian languages (all of which belong to the three language families, Teutonic, Rome and Slav) were gradually formed. Different dialects in the Latin language split into many separate ones, as Europe became some 30 different countries. Today, it is very difficult for a Spanish who doesn't understand English to live in Britain, while their ancestors and those of the British spoke a common language, Latin. Without the help of translation, an Englishman not knowing ancient Latin is not able to understand *Oedipus* or *The Iliad* or *The Odyssey* in the original, although all these books were written in the language used by his ancestors. Indeed, even today, books written in English 500 years ago can be understood only by English scholars, while a Chinese middle school student can basically understand novels like *The Romance of the Three Kingdoms*, *Heroes of the Marshes* and *Pilgrimage to the West*, all written in Chinese characters 500 years ago. With the help of reference books, a qualified Chinese high-school student can basically understand books such as *Historical Records*, which was written 2,000 years ago. Because the relationship between the pronunciation and the form of Chinese characters is not as close as those in alphabetic languages, the pronunciations of ancient and modern characters have continued to change, but the form and meaning of the characters have remained comparatively stable. A contemporary Chinese could communicate with the sages of antiquity. This characteristic of the Chinese language in transcending the ages, expressing both the ancient and contemporary meanings in its characters, has made the language indispensable in propagating Chinese culture.

Though the ethnic and regional groups of China have had many oral languages and there are seven major dialects in everyday use today, by utilizing only Chinese characters one can communicate with any other Chinese. A literate person from Guangdong can easily get around in Harbin, and a person from Beijing who does not know Cantonese, can get along in Hong Kong and Guangzhou as long as he knows Chinese characters. Chinese characters continue to play a very important role in China's ability to maintain a multi-ethnic and unified country. The Chinese writing system is the Great Wall of the people's culture.

Second, Chinese characters are very rich in conveying meaning.

Chinese words are made up of morphemic syllables, combining pronunciation and meaning in one. This feature makes each square-shaped character a unit in which all linguistic information is contained. Each character has three-fold significance — morphology, pronunciation and meaning, presented as one.

Another reason why Chinese words are rich in meaning is the country's long and diverse history. The evolution of the Chinese characters followed the people's

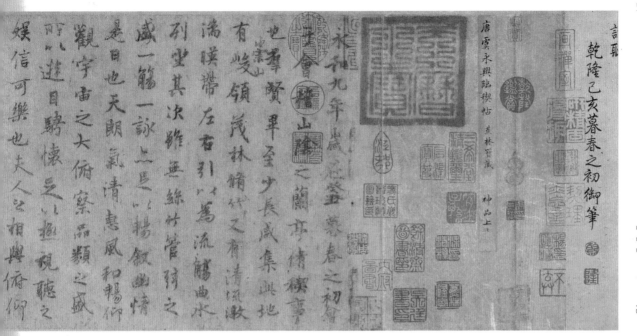

A calligraphy masterpiece by Yu Shi' nan

accrual of information and understanding of their society and the world that surrounded them. All the names of woody plants have a radical component of 木 usually on the left side, while all those of herbs have ⺾ on the top. This is an illustration of the early knowledge of plant taxonomy.

As a written language, Chinese is much simpler than others. A survey showed that among all the printed translations of the of United Nations' resolutions (Chinese, English, French, Russian and Spanish), the Chinese version was always the slimmest.

Third, the Chinese characters have enormous potential for generating derivatives, and forming new words.

There are estimated to be all together 415 syllables in Mandarin, or the standard language, Putonghua. Considering the four tones, the number of syllables is still only around 1300 - this number is much smaller than the number of English syllables, more than 10,000. However, Chinese have many more morphemes, most of them monosyllabic, so there are many morphemes with the same pronunciation. This created the necessity to make more new words. The many radicals and components made it possible to construct enough new shapes — so each morpheme has a unique morphology and structure. This has helped to guarantee the precision of the written language since very early times, and of course, it has also resulted in the creation of a huge number of Chinese characters. Thanks to the proliferation of Chinese words, the richness of the Chinese culture has been preserved and passed from generation to generation.

Many monosyllabic words evolved to become disyllabic ones later. Today, disyllabic words make up the bulk of Chinese words. Many disyllabic compounds are created by either putting together two characters with basically the same meaning, or by using one to modify another, or forming a verbal or noun phrase. These words were created out of the necessity to represent new thoughts. This flexibility, the ability to extend to accommodate new and related ideas, gives the Chinese language its strength.

Fourth, the shapes help to differentiate characters from one another, making them easy to read and memorize.

There are all together eight strokes (一, ｜, 丿, 乀, 丶, 亅, 乛, 丨) that are used to write Chinese characters. There are, however, thousands of ways of employing these strokes to form characters and these characters can in turn form tens of thousands of combined characters. This feature makes Chinese characters easy to recognize and read. Researchers have conducted experiments demonstrating

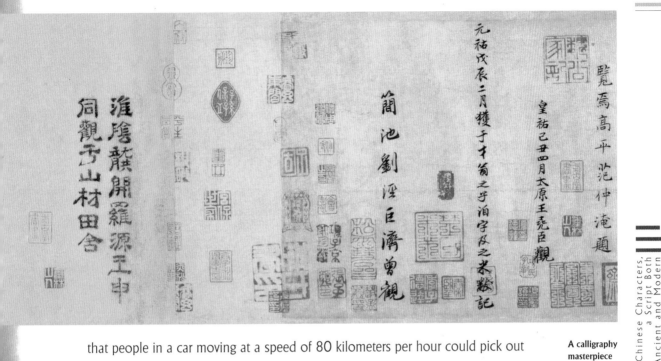

A calligraphy masterpiece

that people in a car moving at a speed of 80 kilometers per hour could pick out Chinese characters on a signpost on the roadside while they could not see clearly the Roman numerals under them. Japanese scholars have shown that it takes less than one thousandth of a second for one to recognize a Chinese character — so Chinese characters enjoy the advantages of condensed information and easy recognition. During the same time period, a reader of Chinese can absorb more information than can a reader of text written in an alphabetic language. In modern science and research, about 30%-40% of one's time is spent in reading, so it appears that the potential of a wider application of the Chinese language will be increasingly recognized.

Many square-shaped characters look like drawings that stimulate quick recognition - this fact makes it easy for them to be understood and retained. In fact, many Chinese characters have such vivid and suggestive structures that the imagination of the reader is stimulated with a mere glance. For instance, such words as 孕 ("pregnancy"), 岩 ("rocks"), 跳 ("jump"), all have evocative shapes. This is an advantage not found in other written languages.

Fifth, reading Chinese characters engages both hemispheres of the brain - serving as a tool to develop the right side of the brain.

According to research by neuro-psychologists, the human brain uses phonetic codes in deciphering alphabetic languages, but calls for the deciphering of both phonetic and pattern codes to understand Chinese characters. Phonetic codes are processed mainly in the left hemisphere of the human brain — alphabetic languages are understood only after this process. It is not necessary to decipher pattern codes with the phonetic process: the meaning of the word is understood through reading the shape or pattern of the word, utilizing the right hemisphere of the brain. Since each Chinese character represents a pronunciation and a meaning, it requires both hemispheres to work together in order to understand it. It is believed that practicing Chinese calligraphy demands more intense involvement of the right hemisphere of the brain, so some scholars regard this is as an advantage, in that it helps to balance the work of the two hemispheres of the brain.

Sixth, calligraphy, the art of writing Chinese characters, is unique among languages.

It is an art that was developed during the evolution of the Chinese written language. In both handwriting and printing, Chinese characters may be lined horizontally or vertically on the page, starting from the left or the right. This freedom is not generally available in alphabetic languages.

In ancient times, calligraphic works were usually written or inscribed on animal bones, bronze ware, bamboo or silk. In modern times, they are rendered on paper. A brush pen, *xuan* paper and water-soluble ink are the three essential elements for Chinese calligraphy, and artists have developed various techniques in their writing, to harmonize the effects of the three elements. Many a masterpiece has been created. Some have been passed down and well preserved to today. Besides the anonymous writers of inscriptions on oracle bones and bronze ware, there were great calligraphers from the Han and Wei periods onwards such as Wang Xizhi in the Jin Dynasty, Yan Zhenqing, Liu Gongquan, Ouyang Xun, Yu Shi'nan, Chu Suiliang, Zhang Xu and Huai Su in the Tang Dynasty. After the Sui and Tang

Dynasties, there were Su Shi, Huang Tingjian, Mi Fu and, Cai Xiang in the Song Dynasty, Zhao Mengfu in the Yuan Dynasty and Dong Qichang in the Qing Dynasty.

There are four artistic features of Chinese calligraphy — structure, strength, rhythm and spirit.

Structure refers to the overall layout of one piece of work and the shape of each individual character. A good piece of work should have a character of its own and inspire a sense of beauty. Looking at a piece of calligraphy by a scholar, the audience should be able to read from it the character and personality of the calligrapher.

Strength or "force of strokes" is the requirement for forming the lines and strokes of a piece of work. It is regarded as inferior calligraphy if the lines and strokes are loose, thin or unbalanced. A kind of inherent strength must be conveyed by the brush. This conforms to the Chinese ethic that stresses uprightness and strength in personality and personal character, so it is an important criterion for evaluating a piece of calligraphy.

Rhythm denotes a harmonious relationship between individual words, lines and the whole piece. All these elements must be connected with one another, forming one integrated body. A character must stand alone, but it is never isolated from the rest of the piece. The space between lines may be wide or narrow, but the connection is always there. It rises and falls and has a well-modulated rhythm.

Spirit is the overall message conveyed by the other elements — it is the overall impression created by the piece of work. It allows the onlooker to identify — and resonate — with the artist.

The beauty of Chinese calligraphy lies also in the education, personality, and attitude to life of the artist. The calligrapher expresses himself without drawing attention to himself. The calligraphy must not be overdone or be aimed to impress and flatter the audience. The artist works purely out of a love for the Chinese characters themselves. Calligraphy also demands a high level of technical skills. It is not easy.

In fact, Chinese calligraphy has much in common with its philosophy and ethics — love of nature, simplicity and strength. It serves as a mirror of their inner minds and spiritual pursuits. Calligraphy is not merely a writing skill, but becomes a means to perfect one's moral quality.

Of course, this magnificent language has shortcomings. For instance, the sheer number of characters is daunting. There are 2,500 commonly used Chinese characters in the *Everyday Chinese Character List*. Another 1,000 characters are often employed too. This is not a small number for anyone who wants to study the language. The complicated shapes and structures frequently intimidate the beginner. Pronunciation is not easy. Only one fourth of the mutually explanatory and pictophonetic characters have pronunciations readily suggested by their shapes and structures. Things are made worse because

A calligraphy masterpiece by Feng Chengsu

of the abundance of homophones. Also, the meanings of words are frequently obtuse. Because of its long history of evolution, one word may have picked many extended meanings - this fact sometimes makes it difficult to understand in a given context.

But the four shortcomings related above are often intertwined with the advantages of the characters. For instance, if not for the complexity in structure and shape, Chinese would not be able to metamorphose new characters so easily. If the pronunciation of all the characters were determined solely by their component parts , one word would have many pronunciations, one for each dialect. If this were true, the written language would not have remained basically stable over the ages. Most importantly, while building on this basic stability, the language continues to evolve. It is clear that the language's advantages override the shortcomings. The future of the Chinese written language characters remains positive, inspiring optimism.

三

The Future of
Chinese Characters

The Chinese characters have existed for thousands of years of changing conditions. During their long history, they were regarded as near-sacred items, respected by all. More than a hundred years ago, Indo-European languages were introduced to China. In modern China [i.e. from mid-1800's to 1919] when education was ignored, science lagged behind, national power declined and the country suffered many disgraces, there arose a popular view that the character-based writing system was one of the root causes for all that. It was said that the system was outdated, and sooner or later, would be replaced by alphabetic language. The advent of the wide use of computers appeared to support this argument. It appeared that Chinese characters were facing extinction.

However, even before the end of the 20th century, major breakthroughs in software development permitting the input of information with Chinese characters gave the lie to that argument. The character-based language is definitely not moribund nor inadequate to the needs of the computer revolution.

That Chinese characters are more legible than alphabetic characters is a well-recognized fact. One recent test of reading ability carried out among first, third and fifth grade elementary school students in both Beijing and Chicago showed that because Chinese students had learned Chinese characters, their reading ability was, in general, higher than American students of the same age who learned English. The initial process of Chinese children learning their language is difficult at first and easier later, while the process of American children learning English is almost the opposite. This bi-cultural investigation demonstrated the advantage of the Chinese language in being more easily read than another language. This writing system is surely capable of meeting the requirements presented by the information age now, and in the future. This highly stable system has passed the test of time, and is fit to continue to preserve China's history and culture far into the future. The characters' powerful ability to produce derivative characters has made them uniquely adaptable to describing future scientific developments.

Linguistic scholars assert that first, because Chinese characters employ a single syllable, as opposed to alphabetic languages, they have a strong ability to retain the integrity of their meanings. That is why the sound of Chinese characters is readily susceptible to spectral analysis and processing. Second, as a single Chinese character can be written in a thousand styles, it is easy to identify technically. Third, the logic of the combining of Chinese characters to form new words easily accommodates modern science: the characters possess an unlimited ability to combine new words, to express new scientific thoughts and discoveries. Fourth, Chinese characters, which have only 415 syllables, appear to be more suitable than the English language, with its 10,000 syllables, in computer-based voice-recognition programs. No matter how science advances, and no matter what new morphemes appear, the Chinese language will always be able to adapt to, and express them. The written Chinese language holds a vast amount of information inside the configuration of its strokes. Its advantage in transcending the different dialects is unique.

The Traditional
Worldview,
Chapter Five
Ethics and Morals

China is a country that is at once ancient and young. China's civilization, the world's longest uninterrupted civilization, is both traditional and modern. Since its birth, it has never succumbed. The core of the Chinese civilization is its very traditions of its outlook on the world, and the moral values underpinning Chinese society.

—

The Traditional Worldview

What is the world and the cosmos? What is the relationship between man and the world? This is the basic question of Chinese philosophy. Virtually all great Chinese thinkers, from Ji Dan, Duke of Zhou of the Western Zhou Dynasty, to Zhang Taiyan and Dr. Sun Yat-sen in modern times, regarded the solution to the question of the relationship between "tian", or the Heaven, and man as a high priority.

"Pan Gu separates the heaven and the earth." "Nü Wa patches up the sky." These are both mere legends. What is the cosmos really like? Laozi, a thinker during the Spring and Autumn Period, was the first philosopher who tried to explain the cosmos from what can be seen happening in the world, without resorting to supernatural will and power.

Laozi, whose real name was Li Er, was a native of Ku County of the Chu Kingdom (modern-day Luyi County, Henan). The years of his birth and death have not been recorded. We know little about him except that he was once appointed Keeper of the Imperial Archives of the Zhou Dynasty, the equivalent of the Director of the State Library today. He must have read many of the classics and writings of antiquity that were not available to the public, and so acquired knowledge that others could only dream of possessing. Erudite, and with a good understanding of both the advance and decline of many a kingdom and state, he commanded a wide repertoire of historical anecdotes, as well as social etiquette and court protocol. That is why he was respectfully called "Laozi", or Old Master.

Laozi was an older contemporary of Confucius. The latter is said to have once asked Laozi for advice, and Laozi admonished him to follow a modest approach, not to be conceited and not to rush to judgment. Indeed, Laozi could have been Confucius' mentor. Although there were spirited debates between Laozi's Taoist followers and Confucius's literati disciples as to their respective approaches on administering a state, private relations between the two masters were cordial and they respected each other. Later, when civil war flared up under the contention for the throne of the Zhou Dynasty, Laozi traveled westward to Qin to take refuge in seclusion. When he passed Han Gu Pass (located to the southwest of the modern-day city of Baoling, Henan), the governor, Yin Xi, held Laozi and would not release him until he wrote something. It is said that when Laozi finished writing his masterpiece *Laozi*, also called *Daode Jing* (formerly known as *Tao Te Ching* or *Classic of the Way and Virtue*), he packed some provisions presented by Yin Xi, sadly mounted a blue ox and

Right: Laozi riding an ox

left in a state of deep melancholy, through the pass to the west. That was the last anyone saw of Laozi.

According to Laozi, *Dao*, or "the Way", is the source and root of the Earth, Heaven and everything between. The Way has no starting point and no end. "The Way is Nature itself and Nature itself is the Way. "The Way exists by itself and is independent of the will or control of others. It is infinite, ubiquitous and prevails everywhere. The running of the Way is totally free and absolute, following only its own laws but nothing else. The Way gives birth to everything in the universe and all things in the world can trace their origin to the Way. The Way is both the father and mother of the cosmos, of the world".

Laozi thought that the cosmos was formed of a circle, and the inside of that circle was filled with constantly moving *qi*, or vital energy. Everything, from the innumerous galaxies to the tiniest particles, including mountains, plains, trees and animals, is made up of the vital energy in the circle. It is the same as saying that everything in the world is the product of Nature itself. There are no gods, no deities, nor supernatural powers, nothing beyond that of the Way.

Laozhi's book copied on silk

According to this school of thinking, man is also a product and a part of Nature. Laozi said, "First there was the Earth and Heaven, then everything on Earth; when every living creature appeared on Earth, then came man and woman; when there were man and woman, there appeared couples and families."

Laozi borrowed the notion that "The Way follows Nature" to reveal a common yet profound truth: that all things and creatures in the world, including man and his society, have a natural character. So as long as the "sage", or the ideal ruler, follows the Way, then his subjects will behave and cultivate themselves according to their nature and will be obedient in their own places in the world. This is the application of Laozi's preaching of "The Way follows Nature" in everyday life, and in politics.

Ideal individuals make up an ideal group of people. Ideal groups of people make up an ideal society. Ideal societies, together with the perennial and ever-living Nature, make up an integrated universe. This is China's ancestral vision of an ideal world.

It could be logically inferred from the concept "The Way follows Nature" that humans must obey the law of nature and should not put incessant demands on Nature.

Thus, all words, acts and decrees against the laws of Nature are wrong and will bring catastrophes and destruction to human society. So it has become a mainstream rule in the traditional Chinese outlook on the world to "obey the laws of Nature and follow human desire." It is also an important ideological cornerstone of the architecture of China's culture.

It is an essential idea in Chinese culture to pursue harmony between the Heaven and man, or Nature and society. A logical conclusion of this notion is to worship the Heaven, to protect the multitude: this is deeply imbued in Chinese culture. Since early times, Chinese philosophy has regarded humans and their affairs as having been an integral part of the world. Mankind and their affairs have always been regarded as an essential part of the Heaven and Nature, rather than being mere slaves of it. This human-based philosophy is at the base of traditional Chinese culture. However, the word "man" in Chinese culture in most cases has a collective denotation, having virtually the same meaning as "the masses" or "the multitude". It has a rich connotation and color of "the people" instead of "the individual". So it is an important task for the Chinese to learn and absorb the concept of "humanism" that characterizes modern Western culture. Such ideas as "liberation of the individual personality" and "the human rights of the individual" can be borrowed to enrich Chinese culture.

The harmony between Nature and man demands that humans follow the laws of Nature, rather than acting against them. The destructive exploitation of Nature has never been approved. Zhuangzi (c. 369-286 BC) dreamed of a society in which man lived in harmony with birds, animals, insects and fish in a natural environment of mountains and rivers, trees and grass, and in which man and

Nature kept close to each other and developed together in a perfect partnership. Those ancient Chinese sages taught ages ago that man and other living things coexist in one large, common family, with the name of Nature.

It would be an exaggeration to place the theories of Laozhi and Zhuangzi side-by-side with modern environmentalism. However, it is undeniable that the idea "The Way follows Nature" contains elements of wisdom that address to present-day concerns.

The theories put forward by Laozi and Zhuangzi were an early expression by China's ancestors of what an ideal society should be. Further, their theories also represent great achievements in the study of the relationship between man and Nature.

The dialectic way of thought is another important characteristic of Chinese philosophy with respect to its outlook on the world. The early sages who wrote *The Book of Changes* in the Zhou Dynasty realized that the universe is made up of two opposing extremes, and that minor changes could lead to great ones. "The building of a nine-story pavilion begins with consolidating the base, while a thousand-*li* journey is started by taking the first step." "Good fortune lieth within bad, and bad fortune lurketh within good." Those well-known sayings of Laozi are used in modern Chinese, adding color to the language. His junior, Zhuangzi, inherited and continued this idea and wrote "security and threats change places; bad and good fortune breed one another." He went further, carrying this idea to the extreme of regarding everything as a transient phenomenon, falling into a pit of relativism and fatalism. His famous, beautifully-written "Butterflies and Dreams" is a good illustration of this idea.

Dialectics is still an important tool in thinking, not only in philosophy, but also in science. Scientists and researchers today still base their work on the notion that the world is made up of opposing forces, and the balance of these forces determines the world around us.

Theories of an Ideal Society

Each of the hundred schools of thought that sprang up during the Spring and Autumn Period raised its own ideas of an ideal society.

For Laozi, his utopia was described as this: "Let your community be small, with only a few people; keep tools in abundance, but do not depend upon them; appreciate your life and be content with your home. Sail boats and ride horses, but don't wander too far; keep weapons and armor, but do not employ them in aggression. Let everyone read and write; eat well and make beautiful things. Live peacefully and delight in your own society; dwell within the cock-crow of your neighbors, but maintain your independence from them." Laozi thought that it was best for the ruler or the government to do nothing and just let Nature follow its course. He said that "to do nothing is actually to do everything." A good ruler should do nothing but let people care for their own interests.

Zhuangzi reiterated Laozi's idea and carried it further by advocating that one "follows the natural way" totally, without reservation.

For Mozi (c. 468-376 BC), philanthrophy and non-aggression should prevail in a utopia. Philanthropy means to love each and every one, with everyone being required to "contribute a little love to the world". War and conflict would be inevitable if there were no mutual love and philanthropy. Thus, non-aggression is required. When there is no fighting, man must love one another. "Mutual love leads to mutual benefit". The ideal of philanthropy had as its banner-carrier Mozi, in China, more than 2000 years ago.

Hanfeizi (*c.* 280-233 BC) advanced the idea of combining law, politics and power to create an ideal society. He advocated ideas like, "the law does not bend before the powerful," and, "punishments and rewards should be equal for ministers and commoners alike", making him the earliest promoter of the doctrine that all are equal before the law. Kings and emperors should learn the art of politics, while ministers, officials and the people should all obey the law. Behind politics and law is the Ruler. The Ruler should be able to employ political chicanery to rule his subjects, as the rule of law applies to his subordinates and the multitudes, but not to himself. In Hanfeizi's ideal society, the people have to tread a careful line in obeying the laws, as it is for their benefit, but above them is the supreme Ruler.

Mainstream thought about the ideal society of China is contained in the theories of Confucius.

For Confucius, a world of great harmony would be a society made up of many individuals acting rationally, organized around a series of societal orders. In this unified and harmonious society, everyone would contribute his talent and efforts, and in turn, be taken care of from cradle to grave. Everyone would live happily in this society.

Confucius (551-479 BC), had the first name of Qiu. His ancestors were originally aristocrats in the Song Kingdom and later moved to Zouyi in the Lu Kingdom (a place southeast of the city of Qüfu, in modern-day Shandong) to take refuge. His father died when he was three years old, and at the age of seventeen, he lost his mother. Confucius's early years were miserable. Although he was later appointed Minister of Justice, along the way he served as a warehouse keeper, a supervisor of shepherds, an orchestral player - and maybe - a conductor.

He understood the beauty of music and later listed music as one of the Six Arts. He placed poetry, which could be "sung", at the top of the list. Confucius was not only a philosopher, a politician, an educator, but also an artist.

Etiquette and benevolence are integral to the social theories of Confucius. Etiquette not only has a lot to do with political power, but is also a guide to personal behavior: It is the actualization of the world of great harmony. Confucius studied the rituals and etiquette of the Xia, Shang and Zhou Dynasties, and made efforts to modify them. The Zhou rituals advocated by Confucius were actually ones that had been modified by him. The protocols and rituals he taught had been adapted to suit the requirements and demands of the circumstances of the society of that time.

A portrait of Confucius by Song Malin

Benevolence is the supreme virtue, and embraces the soul of courtesy. It serves as a standard when one person relates to another. Benevolence requires mutual love and respect. As the center of the supreme paradigm in the theories of Confucius, it is the core concept that constitutes the framework determining a person's outlook on the world and life, ethics, personality, psychological structure and moral standards.

How on earth is a world of great harmony to be realized?

Confucius taught that a set of orders and norms must be established. "Let the ruler be the ruler, the subject the subject; let the father be the father and the son be the son." From the top ruler, to his ministers, to fathers and to sons, everyone must behave in a manner appropriate to his position and follow an ordained set of rules and guidelines. No word may be uttered, nor any behavior in breach of these rules and guidelines be contemplated. "Personal desires must be suppressed and the etiquette and rituals must be kept intact." Confucius said, "To discipline oneself to fulfill rites is benevolence." He also said, "The day all the rites are fulfilled in self-discipline, all under Heaven will have benevolence." So benevolence is obtained when everyone behaves himself by following self-discipline and social guidelines. "A benevolent person loves his fellow men." A harmonious society will appear when everybody suppresses his private desires, and obeys the disciplines guiding social order.

The stricture of "Let the ruler be the ruler, the subject be the subject, the father be the father and the son be the son" serves the ruling class well. However, when the ruler does not follow the stricture, implicit is the justification to dethrone the despot. Mencius (c. 372-289 BC), one of the greatest Confucian scholars, later raised such popular notions as "the ruler is not as important as the people" in addition to adhering to Confucius' idea of "benevolent politics" and "social etiquette". Mencius said, "The interest of the people comes first, followed by that of the state; that of the ruler is least important". In addition to placing the importance of the ruler behind that of the people and the country, Mencius also upheld the idea that, "It rightly serves him, the despot, to be eliminated." In the ideal society envisioned by the followers of Confucius, there is no tolerance for harsh politics and despotism. Instead, it is an orderly society characterized by harmony, benevolence and courtesy.

Confucius did not see his dream of a world of great harmony realized in his lifetime. He assumed the capacity of teacher from the age of thirty; it is said that he had 3,000 disciples — among them 72 were his favourites. He conducted a tour of the kingdoms with his disciples and followers to promote his ideals, but to no avail. In his old age, he returned to his home to complete his writings. His efforts in sorting and compiling ancient texts contributed greatly to the preservation and development of China's cultural heritage.

Confucius died at the age of 73. He was China's first thinker who achieved world fame.

≡

Traditional Ethics
and Moral Values

The early sages in China believed that the family was the basic element of society. Since a family is bonded through blood, the relationship between father and son is the core of the relationship (the prominent feature of a patriarchic society). This relationship is extended further, to encompass relationships between husband and wife, monarch and the subject, senior and junior and between friends: these are called the Five Cardinal Relationships, and they include most of the relationships between people in a society.

The Five Cardinal Relationships of the Chinese have been evolving, adapting and showing new significance over the ages, as society and the economy develop. Nevertheless, the principle of harmony and the standard of benevolence have always been held as basic concepts. Between the Five Cardinal Relationships, unity and harmony are always upheld as the absolutes. Mutual respect and love are central to the Relationships.

A man assumes more than one role in his position in society. A father is someone else's son, and a senior is a junior before an elderly person. Thus a man must be able to follow many codes of social conduct and values, and must shift his roles, his behavior and manner of speaking, under different circumstances.

Harmony between the Five Cardinal Relationships is the cornerstone of a harmonious society. The value standards of its ethics establish a benchmark of morality. It is immoral to act against the established ethical standards, and society will denounce and punish offenders. These deeply rooted ethical concepts have played a great role in maintaining a set of firm and high moral standards over thousands of years. For instance, it is always a great offense to go against the will of one's parents, to act with disrespect to elders, to be ungrateful to one's friends - these are universal values, regardless of the social system. These are at the heart of one's ethical heritage and traditions.

Strict ethical and moral standards have nurtured many an outstanding person. "Be the first to worry about the affairs of the state, and the last to enjoy oneself." "Do not indulge yourself in power and riches, and do not waver when stricken by poverty and obscurity; you will then not surrender to strength and might." These were the teachings of sages in the past, and many national heroes have taken them as their mottoes.

Confucius put forth benevolence as the highest standard of social ethics and the nation's moral benchmark when its welfare is at stake. He hoped that it would become the moral code for the Chinese people. It is clear that the people received this idea with enthusiasm.

Mencius has taken Confucius' principle further, and raised the notion of righteousness as the core value and the supreme standard of ethics. His proposition has been adopted as the moral guideline governing state affairs, for the past 2,000 years.

Confucius' concept of benevolence led to the denunciation of depots. From the principle of righteousness enunciated by Mencius, it has been inferred logically that "It rightly serves him, the despot, to be eliminated".

Confucius is giving a lecture.

For Mencius, upholding righteousness was the highest form of courage and morality. One should even be willing to give up his life in order to keep the principle of righteousness intact. Thus to die for the cause of righteousness has come to exemplify the most courageous act for an individual. A man doing this is considered a noble character; a nation with many such people is a great nation.

For Mencius, among the five fundamental moral principles — benevolence, righteousness, courtesy, intelligence and faith, righteousness was the core value. Righteousness implies justice and moral principles. Although the interpretation of these principles may change from time to time, the basic values stay intact. "To die for the cause of righteousness" implies that life is secondary to the principle. This is an immortal notion in Chinese culture. Upholding righteousness has been one of the essential moral standards for the Chinese; this is in contrast to the principle of personal interest first.

However, there is more to be desired in Chinese ethical values. For instance, many say there should be a sixth dimension of relationships, that between the individual and society in general. There are proponents who say that Chinese have high private moral standards but low public discipline. So the sixth relationship, that between a citizen and society, should be strengthened.

Chapter Six

A Traditional and Unique Way of Life

In 1920, the British philosopher Bertrand Russell visited China. He used the characteristics of Chinese ways of life — peace, steady advancement, industry and frugality — as a disproof of the ways of Western countries. His observations did not cover the entire spectrum of the Chinese way of life, but correlated fairly closely with China's historical traditions.

Briefly stated, the center of the Chinese way of life is harmony and order.

—

The Family — The Center of the Chinese Way of Life

The relationships among individuals, families (extended to clans) and society are a basic issue that every society must come to terms with. If one considers the historical practice of Western countries, it appears to center on the relationship

Left: Celebrating the Lantern Festival

147

between individuals and society, lacking the interim link of family. In contrast, the important relationship in China is that between the family (or clan) and society; this approach gives less prominence to the inclusion of the individual. The development of human society everywhere appears to confirm that these three must all be present: that the ideal society provides for harmony and order among the individual, the family and society.

The traditional Chinese way of life, in theory, advocates the harmony and order among the individual, the family and society. The best way to accomplish this ideal is to "cultivate one's mind, manage a family well and efficiently govern a country." However laudable the ideal, this approach has, in its practice, encountered many obstacles.

In traditional Chinese culture, the family is the basic unit of society. All of society is seen as the extension of families, while individuals are only one part of the family, and more often than not, they are not respected as independent units. In Chinese ethics, the blood relationship between the father and son is the most important element of society. Therefore, Chinese

families in fact are small groups with the blood relationships between fathers and sons being at the core. The extended families of old had "four generations living under one roof" or "five generations living under one roof". While modern families increasingly include only two generations living together, the tradition and the ideal of four generations living together still remains. The so-called "four generations under one roof" meant the cohabitation of the father and mother, son and daughter-in-law (or daughter and son-in-law), grandson and granddaughter-in-law, the great-grandson and the great-granddaughter.

"If the family lives in harmony, all affairs will prosper" and "manage a family well" are principles that extend to "effectively governing a country": these are traditional Chinese ideals. As long as the family is peaceful, stable and happy, then society too will enjoy peace and prosperity. This seems to have become a universal truth. Even today, a warm and harmonious family meets the most basic personal needs, and remains the ideal of Chinese people.

Every member of a Chinese family is a component of this order. Each one plays several roles, and every role has its own code of conduct and moral ethics.

Parents are at the same time sons and daughters, as well as descendants of further lineage, and the wife is to the husband as the husband is to the wife. The family establishes a model of respecting the elderly, cherishing the young, loving, respecting and caring for each other. At the same time, all are part of a larger society, and must demonstrate the qualities of professional dedication, diligence, modesty, self-respect, self-support, managing one's family well, and adhering to one's faith. Only by demonstrating these qualities to one's children, can one expect to see the development of model citizens. For that reason, family education has long been emphasized by the Chinese people. Being criticized as "without proper family education", or "lacking family education" has always been the greatest expression of disapproval.

The aim of order is harmony. In a Chinese family, the hierarchy of the elders and the young creates an atmosphere of harmony, warmth and unity, one that includes remembering and respecting one's forebears. The family looks to the future with care, cherishing the young, while at the same time addressing the present. Any speech or conduct that is seen as inconsistent with this atmosphere is regarded as inappropriate, and is subject to the reprimand of all members of the family. Chinese people pay attention to the positions and roles of all members of the family, and insist upon maintaining harmony among all.

Families evolved into clans, and clans further evolved into communities. One of the forces of coherence of the Chinese nation is the bond of clans. The idea of tracing back one's ancestry is still the most powerful centripetal force of the Chinese nation. Putting emphasis on the family is a time-honored tradition of this nation that has lasted for thousands of years. A distinguished ancestor will bring pride to his descendants for thousands of years. The many descendants of eminent leaders will not sully the name of their ancestors no matter what the consequences. Thus the harmony and stability of families and clans are the assurance of peace and the advancement of society.

Unique Diet and Health

The extensive range of the Chinese menu is a product of the country's history. Since society's food-procurement activities evolved from fishing and hunting to animal husbandry and to farming, the menu encompasses both animals and vegetables. From the sea, lake and river, from the mountain and the sky, from the cave to the forest to the plains, come an abundant variety of foods for the Chinese table. It is said that "eating and having sex are human nature." These are two major requirements for maintaining the continuance of the human race and its society. The Chinese culture emphasizes eating, while the Western culture stresses sex; each has its advantage. As a result, after thousands of years of development, Chinese cuisine has reached a state of perfection.

For Chinese people, dining is one of the most pleasurable activities, best exemplifying harmony and order. The convention followed at the Chinese table is the use of round objects: diners are seated around a round table, dishes are served on round plates, in round bowls and teacups. Circular shapes, rather than sharp and hard angles, suggest reunion and harmony. However, the round table also permits seating by hierarchy: elder and younger, senior and junior, guests and hosts. When being seated for a dinner, elders, and senior and important guests are the first to be seated. After them are the children, who enjoy special attention, and sit shoulder-to-shoulder with the elderly. The order is a representation of social ethics. The meal is accompanied by formalities such as making toasts, positioning the dishes, urging servings of special food and drink upon guests, and changing dishes, and all these formalities are centered around the senior attendees. There are other ways to configure a dining table: while the round table emphasizes the feeling of reunion, the square "Eight Immortals" table emphasizes the relative positions of superiority and inferiority of the diners. Its atmosphere is very solemn and formal, as opposed to the happy ambience produced by a round table.

Chinese dishes have reached the height of perfection. Established rules of etiquette include the matching of various dishes and utensils, and the sequence of serving the dishes. Also, there are less formal activities — playing a drinkers' wager game, guessing riddles, the "finger guessing" game and singing songs. All of these have connections with Chinese culture and art. Worthy of mention is the live performance by the chef, cutting and slicing the presentations at the table in front of the diners. For each dish, the chef employs cutting, slicing, carving and engraving techniques. Every course is worthy of careful appreciation: diners at once appreciate the artistic beauty of the presentation on their dishes, as they savor the taste of the magnificently-prepared food. Dining is also an occasion for the Chinese people to exhibit their ethics, their values, and their attachment to their families — the atmosphere created by such a meeting is especially moving. Many wandering Chinese long, day and night, to sit beside their parents once again, to savor a meal cooked by their mothers, to enjoy the tender affection of the occasion.

China has always paid great attention to cuisine: it sees cooking as analogous to governing a country: "To govern a large country is like cooking many small dishes". Politicians gain inspiration on how to effectively govern a country from

the techniques of cooking. People regard food as their prime want. Chinese cuisine has been strongly influenced by the country's philosophy and culture, but it has additionally become an independent art which has been shared with the world. Chinese dietary culture has always been promoted and developed by literati and artists. They used their own erudition and imagination to create dishes to contribute to the culture, leaving to the world delicacies like "Dong Po Pork" created by Su Dongpo, and "stir-fried diced chicken with chili and peanuts" created by Ding Baozheng, an official of the late Qing Dynasty. Many home-made dishes, illustrating independent styles of cooking, have asserted themselves as part of the nation's cuisine. If a person, even one possessing great knowledge, did not understand the art of cuisine and was unable to cook a few dishes competently, then he will be regarded as being lacking. He is not well-rounded in his knowledge, in old tradition.

Chinese dishes relate to climate, and season and ceremonial holidays. Fish should be eaten during the Spring Festival, because it suggests surplus or abundance, for fish and surplus share the same pronunciation in the Chinese language. Eating dumplings means "bringing in money and treasure", while eating New Year cakes promises "being promoted every year". Eating moon cakes during the Mid-Autumn Festival signifies the "reunion of the whole family". Dumplings should be eaten when receiving guests, while noodles should be eaten when seeing guests off. Noodles are also eaten on an older person's birthday — the noodles are called "noodles of longevity", so the longer the better. It is reported that Marco Polo brought Chinese noodles back to Italy (this has been confirmed by historical records), which later became the well-known spaghetti.

The concepts of "heaven and the people are one" and "I am intimate with each and everything" have sanctioned a very broad approach to the selection of things to eat. One should not mock the Chinese people for their eclectic appetites. Daring to dine on anything edible as a source of nutrition is a reflection of their intelligence and courage. A well-established and dietary culture is the hardest habit to be changed. This is one of the coherent elements of the Chinese nation.

A very important part of the Chinese way of life is preserving one's health. One important idea in Chinese traditional culture is that medicine and food are of the same source. So, many health-giving "medicines" are on the daily menu. They include not only woodland flowers, grasses and edible wild herbs, like the peony, lily, Chinese wolfberry, glutinous rehmannia, Chinese angelica, lotus seed, seed of Job's tears, red dates, great burdock, celery and leaves of pulse plants and others, but also the flesh of animals, including fat, bones, blood and internal organs. Turtle soup, including that made from the soft-shelled turtle, is renowned for being both nutritious and possessing medicinal benefits.

There are also the Chinese martial arts — kung fu. Many Chinese practice the exercises of *tai chi*. This is one of the important elements of the daily life of many Chinese people. Chinese tradition emphasizes strengthening oneself. "Use stillness to check movement", and "the combination of movement and stillness" are two important concepts in *tai chi*. The aim of Chinese martial arts is to strengthen both the body and mind (increasing self-determination and self-respect) and to extend friendship. It is one of the ways to cultivate one's mind. Martial arts are not intended to do harm to others, nor does the practitioner use his skills to boast, or to betray his friends or his country. To refrain from doing these things is called "the right way of practicing martial arts." These are the paramount principles that every person who practices martial arts should uphold.

A nation's culture is the result of accumulation of many things over history. In China, the way of eating to preserve one's health is one part of its culture that has been accumulating for thousands of years.

≡

Essence and
Appeal of the Lifestyle

The way of life epitomized by a nation or region can be placed in one of two general categories. In the words of the English philosopher Bertrand Russell, one is "conflict, exploration, ceaseless revolution and dissatisfaction and destruction".

The other is conforming to nature, being flexible and adaptable to change, gradual progress, peace and harmony.

The culture of the Chinese people, as shown in the conduct of their daily lives, closely adheres to the precepts of Taoism. Taoism is inclined to simplicity in all things. The refined state is seen as living in the countryside to commune with nature, to read, play chess, go fishing and stroll in the mountains and beside rivers. These are the pursuits of intellectuals. Everyone cherishes a beautiful scene on a fine day and perfect conjugal bliss. Their thoughts and feelings conform to each season of the year as they become one with nature, acting in harmony with everything on earth, and valuing human relationships.

Since one's life must respect and conform to the seasons, the *jieqi* (seasonal division points in the calendar) must be acknowledged. In accordance with the changing seasons and climatic conditions, one arranges his daily affairs in a way that is harmonized with nature. That is why the customs of the Chinese people are replete with emotions of closeness to nature: going for a walk in the country in spring, appreciating the lotus in summer, climbing mountains in autumn and enjoying the sight of snow in winter. Green grass and fresh flowers mix with the soft breeze and the clear water; red and yellow leaves merge with the tall sky and white clouds, pure snow fuses with the blurry setting sun. All these sights and sensations combine as if ingredients in a savory sauce, full of abundant but different tastes. All these things together combine to become one, and in each season arouse an atmosphere of cheer, and feelings that inspire poetry.

Festivals and *jieqi* are particularly important to the Chinese. People use these holidays to relax from the daily toil and to enjoy life to its fullest. Although the ceremonies marking these days always center on the relationship and harmony between Heaven and Earth, whether it is a prayer for blessings or a sacrifice to a god, the deities are in fact less important than the peace and serenity the holidays bring.

The Spring Festival is the most important public holiday. People grow eager just after *Dong Zhi* (December 21-23). The prelude to the Spring Festival, or *Guo Nian*, starts with the beginning of *La Yue* (the twelfth month of the lunar calendar). *La Ba* porridge must be eaten on the eighth of that month. This porridge is prepared with many types of coarse cereals, beans, and dried fruit, symbolizing a bountiful harvest.

The twenty-third of *La Yue* is *Xiao Nian* (Minor Spring Festival), when sacrifices must be offered to the Lord of the Stove and his wife. He is a rustic deity, whose name, according to some books, is Su Jili (a proverb in Beijing says, "the Lord of the Stove bears the original family name of Zhang. It suffices to offer him a bowl of cold water and three sticks of incense.") Sacrifices to the Lord and Lady of the Stove can be almost anything, depending on how rich and willing the host is. Some people offer glutinous barley candy to bind shut the lips of the Lord and Lady of the Stove so they will not speak ill of humans to Yuhuang Dadi, supreme ruler of all the deities. Cold water, a plate of straw and fodder beans are also usually offered for the horse of the Lord of the Stove. The master of the house will then light three sticks of incense and entice the godly couple out of the dark kitchen by burning paper icons of them in an iron jar. The dancing flames send the couple on their way to heaven to report to Yuhuang Dadi. This is a solemn ceremony and must be performed by a man. Ironically, the ceremony aimed at fooling deities is taken quite seriously.

The following day is the twenty-fourth of *La Yue* and the main task is to clean the house - symbolizing the desire to brush away the old and usher in the new. Over the next two days, the twenty-fifth and twenty-sixth, bacon and other meat must be stewed in order to finish these tasks before Spring Festival to free the stove from being used. On the twenty-seventh chicken and fish are prepared.

After days of lively anticipation, the thirtieth of the month, *Nian San Shi* (New Year's Eve), arrives. Called *Shou Ye* (Keeping Vigil), legend has it that one must not sleep on this night in order to welcome the arrival of the *Nian* (Year). Then all the deities will retire and the Lord and Lady of the Stove will be invited back home. At this time the couple, who have stayed in heaven for seven days and nights, return by the decree of Yuhuang Dadi, with blessings for peace and good health for the household in the coming year.

The Spring Festival ends on the fifteenth of *Zheng Yue* (the first lunar month of the New Year). The final day is called *Yuanxiao Jie* (the Dumpling Festival) or *Deng Jie* (the Lantern Festival). The round dumplings eaten on the day symbolize unity. Dragon and Lion Dances are also performed to celebrate a return to toiling in the fields. During the night of *Yuanxiao Jie*, all sorts of lanterns are lit to showcase the skills, aspirations and expectations of their creators.

Zou Ma Deng (a rotating lantern with pictures) was introduced during the Song Dynasty (960-1279) — a precursor to modern motion pictures. It was also during the Song Dynasty that gunpowder was first used for fireworks. The origin of the Lantern Festival, however, dates back to the reign of Han Wu Di, or Emperor Wu of the Han dynasty, who lived from 156 BC to 87 BC.

During this time, sacrifices were offered to Tai Yi Shen, God of Supreme Oneness, on the fifteenth of the first lunar month of each year. Celebrations would last all night and decorative lanterns and torches were lit to illuminate the parties. After Buddhism was introduced during the Han Dynasty (206 BC-220 AD), the ceremony changed to followers gathering to venerate the light from Buddhist relics. During the Eastern Han Dynasty (25-220 AD), Emperor Ming decreed that "lanterns be lit up for the grace and glory of Buddha" in the royal temple on the fifteenth of *Zheng Yue*. Other emperors continued the tradition. The Lantern Festival has now been celebrated for more than 2000 years.

Right: People making merry in the snow

While the lanterns continue to get brighter and more colorful, their original Buddhist symbolism is fading. Now the lanterns symbolically light our path to the

A lady playing the panpipe

future and fuel our hopes that the coming year will shine as vibrantly and brilliantly as the lanterns.

There is a festival every month after *Zheng Yue*. Some are for *jieqi*, climate change, others for saying blessings, others for showing respect to ancestors, and some for the memory of deceased relatives (ghosts and spirits). *Duan Wu* Festival, or the Dragon Boat Festival, is the exception. It occurs in May and is dedicated to the memory of the great poet Qu Yuan (340 BC-278 BC).

The fifteenth of the seventh month of the lunar calendar is the Festival of Ghosts. People worship their ancestors, inviting their spirits back home to enjoy the company of family members. Worshippers light *He Deng* (river lanterns) on waterfronts across the country. As darkness descends, dots of candlelight flow downstream taking the worshippers' grief for their loved ones with it.

The fifteenth of the eighth month each year is the Mid-Autumn Festival, a time for wanderers to return home. Unlike the ceremony to honor the Lord of the Stove, the salute to the Moon must be led by a woman. People sip fragrant tea, taste good wine, enjoy crab and appreciate chrysanthemums in bloom during this time. Lying under the light of the full moon with a cool autumn wind makes for an experience not easily forgotten.

On the ninth of the following month is *Chong Yang Jie*, when people climb to the highest ground to gaze into the distance and refresh themselves. Today, the festival is also about respect for elders, fostering a connection between the young and the old.

All these festivals help balance work and play while allowing people to get close to nature and enjoy the intimacies embedded in culture and tradition. The joy of these festivals is the steady, measured heartbeat of Chinese life.

Not only in festivals and other special occasions, examples of Chinese culture may be seen in everyday activities of the Chinese. In playing the lute or chess, reading or painting, the important thing is not technique, but rather one's frame of mind when conducting these activities. The aim is to become aware of the human experience, to conduct one's life with rectitude, and to enhance one's overall achievement. The tea ceremony originated in China. It focuses the attention of participants on clarity of thinking and refinement. The original style of playing the lute was accompanied by the burning of incense — to signify sincerity and peace. Nature is emphasized in paintings. The way of playing chess is more abstruse. The appealing part of playing chess does not lie in the triumph, but in the pursuit of lofty goals such as displaying erudition and intelligence amidst change, maintaining calm while facing danger, and indifference to fame and wealth.

Zen Buddhism has had an extensive following in Chinese history; its practice influenced the daily habits of a great number of people. Speaking of the unspoken, and understanding words unsaid, gives rise to a variety of subtle emotions and mental states. Zen Buddhism may be the best way to exemplify the mysterious quality of oriental culture. The spiritual essence of Zen Buddhism upholds nature and the pursuit of peace and serenity.

The lifestyle of the Chinese people is colorful under its façade of simplicity, vibrant under its countenance of peace. This is a way of life that pursues harmony with nature and with others, simplicity, and a feeling of warmth and oneness with all. This is the culture of the Chinese nation that has been passed down for thousands of years, and is what distinguishes China from other countries.

Unparalleled Achievements in Art and Literature

Chapter Seven

A colored earthen bowl from the Neolithic Age

Art is the product of the beauty of the human race. A nation with a long history and a highly-developed culture will naturally have produced abundant arts, rich in beauty.

It is generally agreed that there are six types of classical arts: poetry, dance, music, painting, architecture and sculpture; poetry further gives birth to literary essays, fiction and drama.

China has a long history, with many outstanding men of letters and artists, so all six classical arts flowered in ancient China. Furthermore, because of the gradual influence of such ideas as the oneness of the Heaven and the human world and antithesis and complement in Chinese traditional philosophy, Chinese art is blessed with a deep beauty and vivid imagination. Only by understanding and learning to appreciate Chinese art is it possible to grasp the philosophical thoughts that encompass all the arts, the country's unique worldview and the democratic spirit of advocating nature, peace, serenity and vigor, and understand the Chinese nation.

—

Unrivaled Literary and Artistic Achievements

All primitive art expresses worship of the world, the feeling of awe of natural forces and puzzlement about people's inner selves — giving it a mysterious quality. Primitive art was most likely related to certain kinds of ceremonies, which is why art even now generates a feeling of solemnity and sacredness.

Such enchanting glamour permeates every facet of ancient Chinese art, because Chinese art represents the most earnest pursuit of the simple and the natural.

Dance

In 1973, a pottery basin with colored bands depicting dancing was excavated in the Neolithic tombs at Shangsunjia Village, Datong County, Qinghai Province.

Three sets of dancing figures were drawn around the inner part of the basin; each set has around the verge of the basin five people forming a circle with their hands clasped. This means that as early as 7,000 or 8,000 years ago, our ancestors had already started to express their feelings by dancing, and use it as part of their community activity. At sunset, when the communal fire was lit, our ancestors who had hunted and labored all day began to sing and to dance arm-in-arm to vent their passions and longings: how pure and simple must have been the feelings that they expressed. This tradition is still being carried out by many Chinese ethnic groups.

"Playing pipa in reverse", a masterpiece from the Dunhuang murals

During the Yin Shang period, dance became a main component of ceremonies involving prayer and worship, and was really the center of these ceremonies. Court dance started during that period, and professional dancers who specifically performed for emperors and aristocrats appeared. During the Qin and Han Dynasties, the development of court dance accelerated. Female professional dancers and singers became fixtures of the court; although they performed in many different ceremonies, their main function was to entertain the emperor. Court dance reached its peak in the Tang Dynasty: one can see to this day, from ancient murals and paintings, the splendor of court dancing at that time. Li Longji, Emperor Xuanzong of the Tang dynasty, was accomplished and versatile; he was known for his masterly ability in playing the *sheng*, bamboo flute, *guan* and *xiao*. He was additionally a musical composer and conductor - even a choreographer. Under his enthusiastic advocacy, both music and dance in the Tang Dynasty attained a very high level of accomplishment. Much of the dancing vocabulary in the Tang Dynasty is still in use today; the dancers' "playing pipa in reverse" is a dancing posture unique in the world, and admired by everyone. The influence of Tang Dynasty dance spread as far as Korea, Japan and Persia; one can find even today the charm of Tang Dynasty dance in the dances of those countries.

In the Southern and Northern Dynasties, before the Tang Dynasty, Gao Su, Duke of Lanling of the Northern Qi Dynasty, was an honest and brave general. However, much to his disadvantage, he had an attractive and effeminate face. His good-looking countenance could not intimidate his enemies on the battlefield. So he had made a ferocious-looking *dai mian* (mask) engraved in peach wood, and wore it in leading assaults against enemy lines. Mask-wearing dancers appeared in later ages and they danced the dance of "Duke of Lanling Charging into Enemy Lines", which gradually developed into some very famous, classic routines. Later, in order to promote the dance "Emperor of Qin Breaking Enemy Lines" composed by Emperor Taizong of Tang, (Li Shiming), Emperor Xuanzong of Tang forbade the performance of "Duke of Lanling Charging into Enemy Lines". This dance was later introduced to Japan, and became one of the performances honored by the state; now the ancient dance has found its way back to its motherland.

Chinese dancing includes both martial and civil dances, dancing with empty hands and dancing with weapons — the latter was especially prominent. There have appeared a number of masters utilizing machetes, swords and clubs. Records of these dances appeared during the Han Dynasty (see *The Book of Han: Records of Emperor Gao*). In the Tang and Song Dynasties, dancing with swords featured masters like Great Aunt Gongsun. "Looking at Great Aunt Gongsun Dancing with Her Swords" by Du Fu tells of her skill: "The sword wielded by Great Aunt Gongsun shines and glitters as if nine suns were falling from the sky, shot down one after another by Yi, the ancient warrior; The vigorous movements of her sword look like the lively and rampaging dragon horses of the carriages of ancient emperors; the thrust of the sword is like the flashing stroke of lightning that splits the air; Then, the next moment taken back and held quietly for defense, the sword comes to a stop like the sudden stay of rushing seawater". One account reported that, in addition to dancing with swords, she also used flags and torches. "The Sword Dance", a great melody of the Song Dynasty, even had simple dramatic plots such as "Banquet at Hongmen" and "Story of Great Aunt Gongsun's Sword Dancing". In the more simple folk art, dancers would wield various instruments while dancing, including farm implements like sickles, axes and hoes, as well as items of everyday household use, such as umbrellas, straw hats and scarves. These accompanied and inspired a great variety of dancing routines. Without the waving handkerchiefs, the *yangge* dance of the northeast would not exist, but this style is very rare in folk dancing in the west.

The use of sleeves and their extensions, long scarves, also contributed to unique forms of dancing. The phrase "Long Sleeves Lending Grace to Dancing" is a good summary of the form that has been passed down for thousands of years. It is said that the long silk sleeve dance performed by the master of Beijing opera — Mei Lanfang — had almost 100 movements, expressing a variety of moods and emotions of the characters. Folk dancing was sometimes specific to a region: the lion dance in Hebei and Guandong Provinces (which was divided into the southern and northern schools), the tea-picking dance in Yunnan Province, the flower-drum lamp dance in Anhui Province, the great *yangge* in the northeast, the impressive gong and drum dance in Shaanxi and Shanxi Provinces, the folk dance of women dancing and beating drums at the same time in Beijing. All these have won awards in the world and enjoyed widespread admiration.

In places like Xingjiang, Tibet, Inner Mongolia, and regions in the southwest, northeast and northwest, there are dances performed by minority groups, all of which have different characteristics.

Music

Archeologists excavated the ruins of a Jiang Village which existed 6,000 years ago. One hundred and twenty houses clustered around the village square, and appeared to have been divided into five groups. Three earthenware musical instruments were recovered from the ruins: one of them has two holes, and when played, produces six different tones. Before this discovery, it had been believed that Chinese music utilized only five notes, i.e. *gong, shang, jue, zhi, yu*, which represent respectively do, re, mi, so, and la. The excavation of this remarkable artifact challenged this belief, and showed that music of 6,000 years ago had at least six notes, one of them being the halfnote — an altered *zhi* (fa).

The "Six Classical Arts" at which Confucius was adept included music. He put learning music as one of the important components of education. Music can inspire students to achieve higher moral standards, and to temper their personalities to become well rounded. This concept of combining music, moral instruction and aesthetics inspires educational systems and practices even today.

Jing Ke, who was famous as the attempted assassin of the emperor of Qin, was a close friend of Gao Jianli of the Yan Kingdom. Gao was an accomplished player of the *zhu*. The *zhu* was a kind of lute similar to the *zheng*, but which was played with a small wooden ruler. Gao Jianli played the *zhu* beautifully, without equal; only by hearing his playing could Jing Ke dance to perfection with his sword. Jing Ke's attempt on the emperor of Qin failed. Gao Jianli resolved to avenge his friend. The Qin emperor Yingzhen knew that Gao Jianli also wished his death, but he could not resist hearing him playing the *zhu*, so he had both Gao's eyes put out, and ordered him to come to the court to play. Gao secretly poured lead in his *zhu* and tried to bludgeon the Emperor to death with it in mid-performance, but he failed and was put to death. This story is full of friendship, loyalty, revenge and tragedy, as it depicts the attempted assassination by Jing Ke out of his loyalty to his

Tang tricolor: musicians on camel-back

country, and Gao's act of revenge based on his friendship for Jing Ke. Also, the sentiment of Yingzhen, insisting on hearing Gao's music at the risk of his own life, was also an important contribution to the story. All these elements of courage, tragedy, loyalty, uprightness, in a story permeated by the ancient, melodic and refined sound of the *zhu*, gave inspiration to generations of artists. In modern times, it has even been adapted to the stage and the cinema.

Chime bells from the Warring States Period were excavated in Hubei Province, and were found to be in a perfect state: musicians were even able to play compositions by Beethoven. A large percussion instrument made of stone that was unearthed from the Yin ruins of Anyang, Henan also had a perfect musical tone, with a melodious and resonant sound. The story of "Pretending to Play the *Yu*" (the *yu* is an ancient musical instrument made up of thirty-six pipes) described a scene of the performance of a large band of 300 people in the Spring and Autumn

Period. If the scene of 300 people playing the *yu* didn't exist, how could a person pretend to play it? The excavated chime bells of the Warring States Period prove that the twelve-note octave, including half-tones, was already known and employed by the Chinese some 2,000 years ago. In the Han Dynasty, not only had Han instruments, like the *zhong* (chime bells), *gu* (drum), *xiao*, *di* (flute), *sheng*, *yu*, *zheng*, *qin* and *se* become very popular, but ethnic instruments like the *konghou*, *pipa*, *fangxiang*, *yunban*, *ruanqin*, *tongbo*, *xiegu*, *yunluo* and *huqin* were also introduced. All employed in orchestras, these came to become China's folk instruments. Emperor Xuanzong of the Tang Dynasty mobilized tens of thousands of musicians and dancers for performances, he himself acting as the lead player and conductor. Such a spectacle is hard for even today's directors to imagine. After the Song and Yuan Dynasties, "Fusion Music" made its appearance. Instrumental music and singing converged in a single production along with dramatic speaking. Music in the Yuan Dynasty was divided into the music of the south, and the north. The *Kunqu* Opera originated in the Ming Dynasty, and the Qing Dynasty had its Beijing Opera, which combined many forms of art. The music of these two operas as well as many local operas are treasures of China's music, and are admired worldwide.

Ballads from different places, like the "Hua'er" of the Qinghai and Gansu Provinces, Naxi Ancient Music which lasted for thousands of years in Yunnan Province, folk songs from Sichuan Province and "Xin Tian You" of the northwest, all have their own characteristics. The ballads of Xingjiang and Tibet, and the "second chorus" ballads of the Miao ethnic minority group may all be called treasures of the world.

The *erhu* piece "*Erquan Ying Yue*" ("The Erquan Spring Reflects the Moon"), composed by the blind folk artist Hua Yanjun (the blind man, A Bing), has been regarded as the most outstanding instrumental piece of modern China - easily the equal of other musical masterpieces of the world. One of world's most

Left: "Bamboo and Stones", a scroll by Zheng Xie

prominent conductors today, Seiji Ozawa of Japan, becomes emotional every time he hears "*Erquan Ying Yue*"; his sweat and tears flow when he conducts this classic. When Mr. Ozawa answers a curtain call, he makes a long bow, still intoxicated by the enchanting melody.

China has never had to bow its head to other nations' music — the country has produced great musicians, and a rich history and tradition of music.

Painting

As can be seen from painted pottery excavated from the Yangshao and Majia Kilns (Qinghai Province), the country already had highly-developed painting techniques by the Neolithic age at the latest. The pottery was embellished with

"The Vast Land" by Wang Ximeng

many animal patterns, like flopping fish, running dogs, hopping frogs and crawling lizards. These animal patterns were gradually replaced with abstract geometrical lines, and later became modified into flowing lines, curves, straight lines, ripples and zigzag forms. This progression showed the process of development from realistic painting, to freehand brushwork painting, and then to geometrical shapes and pure lines.

Chinese painting has theories, techniques and styles unrivalled in the art history of the world, and has made unparalleled achievements. The discoveries of ancient rock drawings of the Red Mountain Culture all prove that early Chinese had already started using pictures to express their imaginative thoughts. Colored silk paintings excavated from the Mawangdui tomb of the Han Dynasty, buried some 2,000 years ago, demonstrate that in the delineation of characters, composition and coloring, early Chinese paintings had reached a high level. Paintings of the Han Dynasty are of precise, simple lines, expressing imaginative themes, exerting a profound influence upon painters of later ages. Paintings in the Wei and Jin Dynasties mostly concern

Buddhist themes. Paintings of the Tang Dynasty, whether depicting human shapes and faces or scenery, had reached an even higher state. The "Qian Li Jiang Shan Tu" ("The Vast Land") and the "Qing Ming Shang He Tu" ("Life along the River during Qingming Festival") of the Tang and Song Dynasties all depicted the magnificent beauty of scenes of China, and the vibrant activities of the cities and towns. In the Yuan, Ming and Qing Dynasties, paintings made by the literati were popular. These paintings illustrated the freeness of the artists' minds, reaching an unprecedented state of elegance and profoundness. Artists of different dynasties, like Gu Kaizhi, Yan Liben, Wu Daozi, Li Sixun, Guo Xi, Zhang Zeduan, Zhao Ji, Shen Zhou, Ba Da Shang Ren (Zhu Da), Xu Wei (Xu Wenchang), Zheng Xie (Zheng Banqiao) as well as Zhang Daqian, Qi Baishi and Xu Beihong of modern times, have made their glorious contributions to Chinese painting.

In the Palace Museum of Beijing, the Palace Museum of Taipei and museums of different provinces, many beautiful picture scrolls are preserved and displayed. Public and private collections in Western countries also have many exquisite Chinese picture scrolls and works of calligraphy.

Chinese painting pays great attention to the precision of ink lines, and strives for vividness and contrast. The integration of painting, poetry, calligraphy and seals is unique in the world of art. Today, many Western artists employ this style and technique: they inscribe a painting, add a seal to their work and use foreign alphabet written in the Chinese style. This is a distinctive modern style, much like western food eaten in a Chinese way. Chinese ink and wash painting, and the *ukiyoe* of Japan, constitute the mainstream of oriental painting. Oriental painting and western canvas painting have formed the two main schools of the world's paintings.

Many painters in the world may not be able to create works in the Chinese style, but few of them are unable to appreciate Chinese paintings. This is because Chinese paintings express profound thought and imagination. From the point of view of acceptance aesthetics, they give the viewer the pleasure of participating in the artistic creation and filling in the gaps. In this sense, it is the ideal, the perfect form of art.

Architecture

Most examples of ancient Western architecture are single, tall structures, because their design was influenced by religious thought — single, tall buildings were expressions of humans' admiration of deities residing in Heaven, and showed their longing to commune with them. Those splendid palaces and skyscrapers illustrate the aesthetics and technological achievements of Western architecture. Therefore, many Western architects look down on the aesthetics of Chinese architecture, which lacks stand-alone high-rise buildings. In the thick book *An Aesthetic History of the World Architecture*, only India is mentioned, among all eastern countries.

Many years ago, a German architect came to China and visited Beijing. When he stepped out of the Qianmen Railway Station and saw the Forbidden City in the setting sun, he was surprised and excited to tears. He had never seen such a harmonious tuning of the contours of a city and its skyline. With the golden setting sun as background, he could see the rolling hills and winding city walls combining together to form a magnificent scroll, showing a hint of mystery. After he explored all the compounds in the Imperial Palace, he was totally persuaded of the value of unique Chinese architectural design.

The ancient Chinese concept of Heaven and humans being one, and the sky being round and the land square, are at the center of Chinese architectural aesthetics. Chinese architects never design impressive high-rise buildings to win accolades, but rather try to strike a proper balance, creating harmony among the structures, the surrounding natural environment and the horizon. They use the design and arrangement of the various structures, consistent with their functions, to achieve an overall, artistic effect and a unique rhythm. It may be expansive and majestic, or quiet and spiritual, solemn or natural. Chinese architecture has absorbed many of the aspects of Chinese painting, and has created many unique styles.

Some temples and other religious structures, like pagodas, all play roles in promoting religious doctrine and create a sacred and mysterious atmosphere. These include the Hanging Temple in Shanxi Province, Temple of Heaven in Beijing and the Wooden Pagoda in Ying County.

The Royal Gardens were surely masterpieces of design. However, the beautiful Yuanmingyuan was destroyed by the allied forces of England and France. The Summer Palace used to be an auxiliary garden to Yuanmingyuan. While it cannot be compared to the beauty of Yuanmingyuan, the Summer Palace is much admired in its own right with its long arcades and spacious layout. Seen from above, Kunming Lake and the Longevity Hill precisely form a cosmological diagram with *yin* and *yang* lying opposite to each other. Family gardens in Suzhou also have their own characteristics. These small gardens can express a bigger meaning. The feelings derived from these gardens are boundless. One feels that every Suzhou garden is a poem or a novel with endless meanings.

Of course, there is also the Great Wall; but it is by no means a simple string of long walls built on mountain ridges. Its construction started as early as the Warring States Period. In the Qin Dynasty, different sections built by the kingdoms of Qin, Zhao and Yan were connected. For the 1,000 years from the Han Dynasty to the Ming Dynasty, the construction of the Great Wall never stopped; the Wall itself is history, a symbol of China's national characteristics and spirit.

Sculpture

One can see that many utensils unearthed from the Shang and Zhou Dynasties are really sculptures, and the beautiful patterns on ancient cooking vessels are also works of sculpture. Examples from the Qin, Han, Wei, Jin, Tang and Song Dynasties portray the beauty of the sculptors' skills even more dramatically. The Terracotta Army, excavated from the mausoleum of the first emperor of Qin, is called the Eighth Wonder of the World; its magnificent layout and exquisite and vivid carvings are admired by the whole world. Huge statues of Buddhas, arhats, Bodhisattvas, deities and demons are legion. Grottoes in Yungang, Longmen, Maijishan and Dunhuang preserve many Buddhist sculptures from the pre-Qin period to the Northern Wei Dynasty. When contemporary visitors view these statues, there is surprise at the aesthetics of these creations. During the Song Dynasty, Buddhist sculpture turned from carving from mud and stone to utilising mediums of wood, bronze, jade and iron. The great standing statue of the bronze Guanyin and the Buddhas in the Longxing Temple of Zhengding all show majestic bearing. Buddhist statues which have been carved into mountainsides, like the giant Buddha

A terracotta soldier

Nine-Dragon Screen

in Leshan, Sichuan Province, the stone carvings in Dazu and many other such works, have attracted the attention of sculptors from all over the world.

Among the themes of ancient Chinese sculpture, apart from religion and works done to accompany dead emperors to the afterlife, there also included some works treating everyday subjects. From many regions, one can see human figurines of different styles, figurines of the performers in operas and other people of various identities. Other popular themes were animals: oxen, horses, dogs, pigs, bears, tigers and lions. Figures of humans excavated in Sanxingdui, Sichuan Province, have vivid and unique expressions, while dancing with their long-sleeved dress. In one huge bust, the eyes bulge out more than two feet from their eye sockets, giving it a strange appearance. Some claim that this is the likeness of Ci You, which was sculpted in accordance with his legendary appearance - having "Double Eyes". The heroic young man, General Huo Qübing who died of illness when he was twenty-some years old, was buried in today's Shaanxi Province; the stone carving in front his tomb is unique. Stone lions and statuary of other beasts laid out in various places meant that ancient Chinese cities did not lack urban sculpture. It is said that the stone lions on the Lugou Bridge are countless, which refers to not only the sheer number of them, but the dexterity and exquisiteness of carving as well. The Nine-Dragon Screen in the Beihai Park of Beijing can also be rated as a consummate work of art.

Poems and Prose, Novels and Drama

Chinese poems originated very early in the country's history. Work songs, prayers in religious ceremonies and songs of romantic love could all be both sung and recited. They gradually became written as poems. Ancient myths and legends, the earliest epics, were a great source of the literature of the country.

The sheer number of Chinese poems and poets probably tops the world. The philosophical thought, aesthetic views and unique outlook contained in Chinese poems are admired by literary scholars all over the world. The exquisiteness of word choice and sentence construction also leads the world — no other language is equal to the task.

> 大漠孤烟直，(Smoke billowing straight upward amidst still desert air,)
> 长河落日圆。(and a round sun setting on the river bank by the horizon.)

is an example of improvisational sentence-making: these two five-character phrases not only present a tidy antithesis, but also utilize a refined choice of words, with the words "round" and "straight" making for a richness both in the meanings and syntactical functions of the words. The sentence arouses a feeling of desolation, and at the same time profundity and grandeur. The picture that can be imagined from this poem is vivid, as the poem evokes the desired feeling by recalling the scene. Try to imagine:

> The surging eastbound river is like a long carpet which shoulders the round setting sun, while the boundless desert hasn't one single cloud over it for ten thousand *li* [a *li* is 500 meters]. Over it, a single strand of smoke [someone interpreted it as a tornado] goes straight toward the sky, looking like a huge exclamation mark.

What emotion does the reader feel when visualizing this scene? One "round", one "straight" — two common Chinese characters created an atmosphere that could not be explained by thousands of words.

Classic of Poetry was the first written collection of poems in China. It contains works of perfection that have been passed down for thousands of years. It is said that *Classic of Poetry* was compiled by Confucius and contains three parts: "*Feng*" (ballads), "*Ya*" (poems for intellectuals or aristocrats) and "*Song*" (songs for praying). The opening poem of the book is a love song, which sings,

> Guan-guan go the ospreys,
>
> on the islet in the river.
>
> The modest, retiring, virtuous young lady,
>
> for our prince a good mate, she.

These four short lines contain every element of literature: time, place, characters, plot, emotion, atmosphere and sentence-making and rhyming. Furthermore, it is also a beautiful picture of love: a good lad is courting a beautiful lass on the islet in the center of the river, while a flock of ospreys fly over while chirping melodiously. Is this not a simple scene of life, whose mood is beautifully evoked by the poet? That Confucius chose this moving love song as the opening poem of this book means that he believed poems should be used to express the most real and simple feelings of life. He believed without hypocrisy in sincere love. *Classic of Poetry* contained 305 pieces. Although many ballads and poems were omitted from the compilation, the book is still a precious treasure.

After *Classic of Poetry* came *Chu Ci* (or *The Poetry of Chu: The Songs of the South*) a compilation of the works of Qū Yuan and his followers. Qū Yuan had an unusually rich imagination extending from the clouds of heaven to the pits of hell — his mind sometimes loftily surges on high, and sometimes descends to the bottom of a lake; sometimes he is talking to deities and sometimes conversing with the souls of ancestors. He looks down to ask the land, and looks up to ask the wind. Many of his poems explore large and profound issues, like life and death, the most important issues in philosophy, making him the first person in the history of literature to deal with these subjects. He posed these questions earlier than Dante's *Divine Comedy*, and much earlier than Shakespeare's *Hamlet*. In *Chu Ci*, his wildly arranged thoughts and poems embodying romantic and imaginary themes; accounts of heaven, humans and hell; his three-dimensional exploration and description of the experience of life; and, the surging feeling of love of country and its people, all illustrated the multifaceted and colorful culture of the Chu Kingdom. Qü Yuan's works significantly influenced Chinese poetry of later ages.

Poems in the form of ballads from the Eastern and Western Han Dynasties came after *Chu Ci*. Many simple but vibrant poems are still familiar to today's generation. "A Poem for Jiao's Faithful Wife Written in the Ancient Style", (or "Southeast Fly the Peacocks"), is a tragic love story still read today. Many representative and outstanding sentences, like "southeast fly the peacocks, hesitating every five *li*", are still full of vitality.

Poems of the Wei, Jin, Southern and Northern Dynasties were very popular at that time. The aforementioned Cao Cao and his two sons Cao Pi and Cao Zhi were all great poets. Lines like, "Just like an old horse in the stable dreaming to travel another thousand miles, for a hero, old as he is, great ambitions inside him never die", composed by Cao Cao, have become an outstanding example of Chinese literature. A poem composed by Cao Zhi,

> The bean is crying inside the pot,
>
> underneath the bean stalk burning hot:
>
> we're born of one stock,
>
> why do you lose no time in sacrificing me?

was said to have been composed within the time it took Cao Zhi to walk seven steps. These lines have been extensively quoted in later ages, in order to express the thoughts of a mind full of emotion, and hope that the tragedy of internecine strife will not occur. Ballads were also very popular at that time, and achieved high

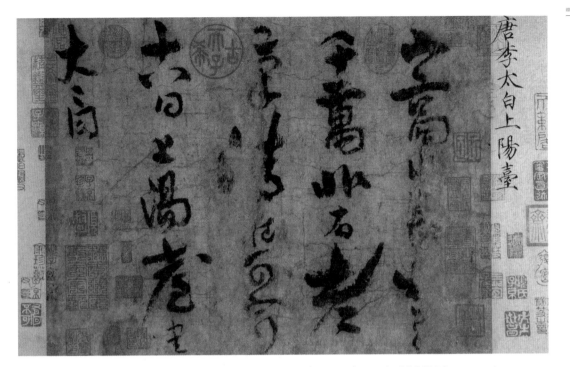

artistic quality. "The Ballad of Mulan" is known in nearly every household. "Chi Le Song" of the Xian Bei minority group expresses the life of a nomadic nation: this song is forceful, simple and clear.

In the Tang Dynasty, a more modern style named *lüshi* (a classical poem of eight lines) developed very quickly. Poems of the Tang Dynasty became the most colorful chapter of Chinese literature, and hold an important position in the whole history of literature. Famous poets of the Tang Dynasty, such as Li Bai, Du Fu, Bai Juyi, and numerous others, left their creativity and intelligence on paper, which has been passed down to today. They raised the Chinese language and its characters to a level of perfection. Their poems will live forever.

After the poems of the Tang Dynasty, there came the Ci poetry of the Song Dynasty. Poets of this age were skilled in the use of alternating long and short sentences. Poets like Su Shi, Xin Qiji, Lu You, Wang Anshi, Li Qingzhao, and Li Yu, the last king of the Southern Tang, all made immortal achievements with their impassioned or sorrowful poems.

During the Yuan Dynasty, the style of poetry changed, and *san qü* (a type of opera with tonal patterns modeled after tunes drawn from folk music) became quite popular. The *san qü* composed by Ma Zhiyuan, Bai Pu, and others are lovely and exquisite. One composed by Ma Zhiyuan is known to almost all Chinese:

Withered vines to a dying tree trunk cling

where a crow perches in the twilight by a stone bridge over the little brook,

there is a house standing alone

beside, a lonely traveler, on a bony horse, travels slowly through a cold wind

from the west along an ancient path that seems to nowhere lead

the sun is about to set below the horizon

who is going to give him, the sad lonely traveler, a welcome tonight?

Starting with the *Classic of Poetry*, Chinese poems strove for artistic mood, meter, and rhyme scheme. Many of these poems are rich with the beauty of painting and music, exuding feelings of passion which profoundly move the reader, and at the same time leaving a lingering feeling which make readers vaguely unfulfilled, still seeking to complete the experience. The wording and construction of the lines of their poems are exquisite. What is more surprising is that, before the birth of the art of film (on December 28, 1895), Chinese poems had already possessed the concept of film, that is, connecting images with sounds in a montage giving rise to emotions, evoking specific, or abstract moods and feelings. Take, for example, the poem "Docking at Night at the Maple Bridge":

Late in the night the moon has gone down

in the sad shriek of the crow as white frost descends blanketing everything

under the sky

the maple trees stand tall by the riverside

only the fishermen's lanterns are still glowing besides mine

I put up for the night in a little boat moored nearby, but cannot sleep when

surrounded by these sounds, scenes and thoughts on my mind

it serves both to comfort, and to remind me of my loneliness and poverty, when

the midnight chiming of the bells ripples to my pillow side

        bells from the Hanshan Temple that is also not within the city of Gusu but
          outside and near.

It is as good as a film montage, with both sights and sounds evoking feelings. Such examples are numerous, and this one is enough to illustrate how beautiful is this artistic method of creating — of arousing strong feelings against the background of natural settings. This approach has had a very long life in Chinese poetry.

After the foundation of the People's Republic of China, three great epics of our nation were excavated and edited. One of them, the Tibetan epic, *The Life of King Gesar,* is 1.1 million lines long. This is the longest poem in the world.

Prose can be called poetry without rhyme. Chinese prose before the Qin and Han Dynasties was mostly concerned with history and philosophy. Works describing the various schools of thought of the Pre-Qin Period, and related historical accounts have been generally of high quality. The unrestrained thoughts, the positive and active writing style, and the beautiful language give these works an important position in the history of literature. Other characteristics, like the meticulousness of the essays by Hanfeizi, and the nimble and spirited prose of Xunzi, represent a splendid showing of skill. *Historical Records*, written by Sima Qian, has been called the outstanding representative of prose of the Han Dynasty. His essays were not only admired by people of later ages, but also praised by novelists and prose writers after him. His achievements have exerted a strong influence on Chinese literature. Another scholar of the Han Dynasty, Sima Xiangru, was also a famous man of letters. The saying "the articles of the two Simas' top the Han Dynasty" originated in ancient times. Prose in the Wei and Jin Dynasties use parallelism liberally, and lay special emphasis on the selection of beautiful words and the forming of symmetrical sentences. Although this style suffers from the defect of formal rigidity, many of these works are regarded as immortal masterpieces. This style of writing also has had a profound influence. "Prologue to the Poem Dedicated to the Pavilion of Prince Teng", written by Wang Bo of the Tang Dynasty, could be called the best

example of parallelism in all six Dynasties. The famous line,

> The sunset glow seems to be flying across the horizon together with a lonely
>   wild duck
> while the autumn Yangtze River flowing beneath the Pavilion shows the same
>   color as the endless sky in the twilight

"Scholars" by
Han Huang

will always be regarded as a pearl of the Chinese language, in its descrition of the physical scene and evocation of emotion. In the Tang Dynasty, Han Yu and Liu Zongyuan originated the classical prose movement, which turned the fashion of emphasizing beautiful — and sometimes pompous — prose to a more simple and natural style. After being promoted by writers like Ouyang Xiu in the Song Dynasty,

189

this movement became a force driving the revolution of literature, making a great contribution to the development of Chinese prose. The eight prose masters of the Tang and Song Dynasties, and later those of the Ming and Qing Dynasties, all made significant contributions, leaving many famous works for posterity.

Western novels and dramas mainly come from epics, while Chinese novels mostly derive from the scripts of street performers. Many professional storytellers made contributions to Chinese novels, as their stories were close to everyday reality and so contained lessons and examples to be followed. Legends from the Tang Dynasty and storytellers' scripts in the Song Dynasty had already taken on an embryonic novel form. In the Ming and Qing Dynasties, Chinese classical novels became fully mature. The famous *Three Collections of Short Stories* ("Stories to Enlighten the World", "Stories to Warn the World", and "Stories to Awaken the World"), *Two Volumes of Amazing Stories*, and, *Strange Tales from a Lonely Studio* all reached a very high level of development. Long novels, such as *The Romance of the Three Kingdoms, Journey to the West, Heroes of the Marshes, Plum in the Gold Vase, A Dream of Red Mansions, Revealing the Original Shape of Officialdom*, and others are all masterpieces that have influenced the world of literature. *A Dream of Red Mansions*, written by Cao Xueqin, has extremely broad and profound significance. Whether one considers its philosophical inclination, its manner of depiction of many walks of life in society, or the sheer literary acumen, all of these elements have stood the test of time, constant examination and study.

Existing scripts show that Chinese drama during the Southern Song Dynasty had already become mature, and gained even greater development in the Yuan Dynasty. The works of Guan Hanqing of the Yuan Dynasty, and Tang Xianzu of the Ming Dynasty, had already reached a very high level. Dramas like *Snow in Midsummer, The West Chamber*, and, *The Peony Pavilion*, could be called pearls in the history of drama. The great playwright Guan Hanqing created many vivid images of women in his plays, expressing his humanitarianism in a relentless fight against feudalism. He put contentious words in the mouth of Dou E in the play *Snow in Midsummer*: "Earth, you cannot distinguish between right and wrong — how can you be called Earth? Heaven, you misjudged and wronged good and wise people — how can you be called Heaven!" His criticism was aimed directly at the feudal social system and its autocrats. Now, types of dramas from different places of China number over 300, from the "living fossils of the theater" such as the *Nuo* Opera of Guizhou Province (the Mask drama), the Tibetan Opera, and the Pu Xian Opera in Fujian Province, to the so-called state treasure, the Beijing Opera — the whole spectrum is treasures of the theater.

=

China's Unique Aesthetics

As long as one appreciates and examines China's traditional art with care, one is bound to encounter many abstruse questions.

Why are the people' eyes narrowed to a crack on the ancient painted pottery excavated at the ruins of Banpo, while the eyes on the pottery basin from Jiang Village, some 1,000 years earlier, are wide open? Is it because people at first looked at their surroundings with excitement and curiosity, but after 1,000 years, they had to close their eyes to meditate on the world around them? What were the respective creators' thoughts while creating these objects of beauty?

The earliest discovered earthenware was colored: a full set of drawing instruments were found in the ruins of the Jiang Village, which existed 6,000 years ago. They included an ink stone with a lid, a pestle and a stone cup for holding water, and even some cracked, red pigment — the natural ore, ferric oxide. This discovery meant that China's ancestors long ago had experience in the perception and use of color — red as the earliest. However, later, as pottery-making techniques became more advanced, they abandoned the red and stuck to black. That the artistry of the black pottery is superior to that of color-painted pottery is clear. Had these ancient artists perceived richer colors from the blurred black than from a spectrum of colors? Chinese painting pays great attention to black and white, the relationship of dark and light, and the dry and wet of the black ink — could these contrasts have anything to do with the artists' grasp of black as being "the whole color"?

Why did patterns on earthenware become progressively simpler and simpler, until at last only lines were left for the viewer to imagine an extended design?

Who can explain the riddle of the "hanging coffin" of Daba Mountain? Artists from ages ago left their murals at desolate and remote places, letting these exquisite works endure eons on cliffs, in deserts and sandstorms.

Why, among time-honored painting masterpieces, do many only contain a few thin bamboos, two or three twisted plums, a scanty stand of pines, a meager portrayal of fruit trees, a brace of tiny sparrows, or a few scattered feathers? Even with the more compelling images of running horses, the horses are few in number. Though there are also works depicting vibrant and prosperous everyday urban life, none of them can match the simple and delicate beauty of the aforementioned works in artistic achievement and reputation.

Why does Chinese architecture favor upturned eaves, while the structures sit scattered and remote among mountains, water and vast plains? North Mount Heng has a "hanging" temple that sits right on a steep cliff. It has been held there for thousands of years by only a few wooden piles. Why was this forbidden place chosen to build a temple?

One may consider the short poem by Chen Zi'ang, "On Climbing Youzhou Tower": "Where are the sages of the past, and those of future years? Sky and earth forever last, lonely, I shed sad tears!" Why has it been passed down to the present day, and will be recited well in the future? Why is even the single sentence, "Sweeps all of a sudden the gust of wind and the clouds are blown across the horizon," by Liu Bang frequently praised? Even women and children know it well. Why have Li Bai's poems glorifying beautiful landscapes won tributes for thousands of years?

Why are the stage settings of Chinese drama extremely spare and simple, while the actors' makeup and costumes multicolored and complex, and capable of moving audiences all over the world?

Why, in Chinese traditional music, with only a simple bamboo flute, an *erhu* (a two-stringed fiddle) or a *pipa*, can many pieces creating different atmospheres be played? Why should the most praised performances be the "light" ones like "Towering Mountains and Gushing Streams"?

There are many more questions that could be posed.

The unique Chinese view of aesthetics permeates all of the country's art. Since traditional Chinese philosophy has as an ideal attaining harmony between human beings and heaven, and as humans are part of nature, it is appropriate for the Chinese people to pay great attention to the harmony between their own creations and nature. They also emphasize that people's spirituality should be raised to a higher level by the influence of nature. Therefore, the main road Chinese art has followed is basically simplicity. It went from being simple to being elaborate and pompous, and after many stages returned to the simple and natural: but this time, a more refined simplicity. So, Chinese aesthetics sees recovering one's original purity and simplicity as the highest state of beauty. Only if, before creating a work of art, the artist gathers imagination and inspiration, understands all the phenomena on earth from the standpoint of simplicity, and tastes the multicoloured nature of purity, can he claim to possess the spirit of beauty. Therefore, simple and vivid lines — and painting, calligraphy, sculpture, architecture and dance that are born of these — are objects of beauty, along with crude peasant's drawings and mud dolls. As long as it is simple, plain, sincere, and full of imagination, it will be appreciated by the Chinese people. Compare this with Western aesthetics, which stresses the power of man and the solemnity of art. The two are as different as night and day.

Because of this underlying philosophy, Chinese architecture pays attention to the combination of the real and the imagined. The change of scenes as one moves and the evocation of feelings through scenery are all typical of Chinese architecture, which attempts to maintain harmony between the environment and the design.

The short poem by Chen Zi'ang shows the long history that Chinese artists contemplate when facing an ancient, desolate platform at a remote place. They connect parallel scenes with the vertical structure of time, and sigh about the endless permutations of contacts between nature and human society. The artist's sigh reveals the special sense of history of the Chinese people, and that is the reason why the poem is told again and again. The sigh of, "Who was the fortunate one who first saw the moon by the riverside, and when was the time that the moon first shone its light on a man's back?" also illustrates the deep influence of Chinese philosophy in the country's literature. It is hard for a nation without a long history to make such perceptive inquiries.

Chinese actors are capable of symbolizing loyalty, treachery, wisdom and foolishness by donning different types of facial make-up composed of multiple colors and contours. They can also use the movement of their limbs and bodies in flowing lines to express complex emotions and thoughts, to replace the reality of the setting with imagination using abstract expressionism. This is exactly the kind of rich artistic expression that springs from the profundity of Chinese philosophy.

The described process of artistry moving from simple to pompous and returning to simple is a long one. It has become the consensus for the whole nation — this is rare in other countries. This is why no matter what type of Chinese art is under discussion, they all have common characteristics and beauty. Recovering and maintaining one's original purity and simplicity, while upholding nature, vividness of presentation, balance and harmony are the essentials of Chinese art.

Chinese art has several unique points. First, Chinese works of art, especially literature and drama, pay a great deal of attention to moral evaluation. "Preaching from a high platform" refers to the attitude of the author toward characters and events on moral grounds. A moral evaluation of the characters has become the standard on which to identify the good from the bad. Sometimes this approach makes the characters one-dimensional, but the tradition of defining and correcting public moral behavior and mores, therefore intervening in real life, is clear.

Second, while China's works of art squarely face reality and make life-like portrayals, they are also replete with colorful imagination. Chinese artwork, passed down from ancient times, nearly always closely reflects the life of the times, but also employs flights of imagination to express its ideals and dreams. Deities and demons, foreign lands and even utopia are all common vehicles for the expression of ideals.

Third, the artists always maintain a sense of detachment from their creations, being at once inside the art and also outside the art. This sense of distance is one of the unique aspects of Chinese art. No matter what beauty, magnificence, tenderness, sadness or grief, the artist on the one hand stands inside the art- work to evoke these feelings, and on the other hand stands outside to objectively appreciate these created emotions and illusions and to witness their own accomplishments. If one is unable to grasp this sense of "inside- outside" balance when appreciating Chinese art, it will be difficult to comprehend the inner world of Chinese artists.

Fourth, Chinese artwork very much emphasizes stirring the imagination of the audience. The artists try their best to immerse the audience and make them participate in their creations. One taboo in Chinese art is "fullness" — there must be many gaps left in the work for the observer to fill in. So, creating from the angle of "aesthetics of acceptance" is a time-honored tradition. Throughout history, societies composed of Chinese artists and politicians have been many, but societies composed of different schools of art have been only a few. That is because Chinese artists, rather than seeking the approval of their peers, strive for harmony between themselves and the recipients, and pursue the creation of a bond between creators and admirers.

Fifth, Chinese art emphasizes expression, while Western art pays more attention to reproduction. So, Chinese art stresses the creator's perception, understanding and feelings of life, as the artists express their own ideas with their own methods. Therefore, the use of symbolism and abstract expressionism becomes natural.

The Influence of Traditional Chinese Art on the World

Chinese art is part of the art of the world. There is no fixed and finite entity called "world literature" or "world art". The world encompasses different countries, regions and nationalities, and "world art" without the representation of Chinese art would be incomplete. Chinese art has always opened its door to all forms of art. Practically every form of foreign art was absorbed by the Chinese people after having been fused with Chinese art and then reconstructed by Chinese artists. Only after going through this process will the new art form be accepted by the Chinese people; if this process is bypassed, foreign art will find it difficult to gain a foothold in China. This nationalization on the one hand means the continuation of the nation's artistic tradition, while on the other hand means the absorption of foreign cultures and turning them into part of the nation's own. The depth and breadth of Chinese culture was, in the same way, formed by absorbing foreign cultures, and making the best of the merits of its own.

While Chinese art was being influenced by foreign art, it was also influencing the art of other countries.

In modern and contemporary art, quite a few masters have been greatly inspired by Chinese art.

The great artist of the Beijing Opera, Mei Lanfang frequently traveled to Europe to perform. His performance in Moscow in the 1930's amazed Russian audiences — and Russia is a country with a long history of art. The charm of the settings and arrangements, and the varied and gracefully flowing lines of the dances of the maestro's long silk sleeves astounded Sergei Eisenstein, master of cinema and one of the pioneers of montage. The montage syntax of his later productions was similar to the structure and arrangement of Beijing Opera. Eisenstein also admitted that many of his ideas on film design were taken from oriental painting. He came to know that Japanese paintings, of which he was very fond, had their origin in Chinese art.

The Beijing Opera starring Mei Lanfang also surprised the German master of drama, Bertolt Brecht. The simple structure of Beijing Opera and the huge spatial effect it could produce was the ideal form of drama that he had been seeking. He had always been searching the way to make the audience immersed in the plot, and at the same time able to appreciate the beauty of the drama with a clear mind. Now, he discovered that the Beijing Opera had developed various methods to achieve this effect. With the help

of the Beijing Opera, he created the Brecht System, which later became an important school in modern drama.

The great Spanish painter Pablo Picasso believed that a strong, expressive use of color could be seen in Chinese paintings and dramas. In their bold use of color, Chinese artists were able to give inspiration to the whole world of art.

From music, architecture, sculpture and dance to martial arts, Chinese culture is spreading very rapidly in Western countries. Even fashionable dress in the West is seeing a Chinese influence. While some Chinese are pursuing Western things, many westerners are pursuing Chinese things. This may look like "two wagons going on two different tracks", but actually the two tracks are connected. The cross-fertilization and fusion of the Western and Eastern cultures will be an inevitable development.

Left: A tri-color
pottery beauty

Chapter Eight

An
Outstanding
Military Culture

Though the Chinese nation advocates peace, during the long process of unification, the evolution of history and dynasties, and the need to defend against external aggression, wars and internal fighting took place. Every country has its own military tradition, theories of war, and practical knowledge of how to conduct its defense. Chinese traditional philosophical and political theories form the kernel of Chinese military culture.

—

A Unique and Traditional Philosophy of War

On War, written by the Prussian, Karl Von Clausewitz, during the first half of the 19th century is a universally recognised masterpiece on military science and the guide to Western thinking on war. Clausewitz said that war is a violent

Left: A mural: "Sword-Wearing Soldiers"

action, and the function of violence is unlimited. Under the guidance of this theory, many Western military strategists advocated the unlimited use of military power. They selected the appropriate weapons, and advocated total conquest. However, after the advent of nuclear weaponry, many military strategists have had to reconsider the appropriateness of the theory of the unlimited use of violence — unlimited violence may cause self-destruction or mutual destruction. Consequently, the theory of gradual escalation appeared at the end of the 20th century. This theory advocates the concept of winning without fighting.

Winning without fighting is an important thought in ancient Chinese military theory. The one who proposed this, Sun-Tzu (who styled himself Sun Wu), born around 500 BC, was a contemporary of Confucius. His masterpiece, *The Art of War*, is universally regarded as a classic even today.

A second *Art of War* was written by another Sun-Tzu — Sun Bin. Sun Bin was said to be a descendant of Sun-Tzu, and was born some 100 years later. He served as an official in the Qi Kingdom, and is referred to as the Sun-Tzu of the Qi Kingdom in order to distinguish him from the Sun-Tzu who served as an official in the Wu Kingdom. The Sun family was really a family of great military strategists. Thirteen chapters of *The Art of War* were written by the Wu Sun-Tzu (Sun Wu). In April 1972, one copy was excavated from the tombs of

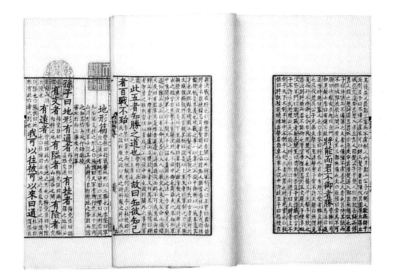

pages from
Sun-Tzu's *Art of War*

the early Western Han Dynasty at Yinque Mountain, Linyi County of Shangdong Province. This masterpiece re-surfaced after being hidden underground for some 1,000 years. This means that the two Sun-Tzu's wrote two treatises on the art of war, both of which are treasures of the Chinese civilization.

There is one sentence in Sun-Tzu's *Art of War* that is admired by military strategists all over the world. "To fight and conquer in all our battles is not supreme excellence: supreme excellence consists in breaking the enemy's resistance without fighting." Sun Wu advocated employing first strategies and then diplomacy to defeat the enemy. These were followed by invasion, and lastly laying siege to the enemy's cities and castles. This outline, the gradual escalation theory, was proposed by Sun-Tzu some 2,000 years earlier than the Western gradual escalation theory, which appeared in the 1990s.

The reason why the Chinese philosophy of war values victory without battles is that the Chinese have a deep understanding of war and a clear assessment of its consequences. Laozi said that *bin* is a terrible thing, and it should not be used by men of virtue unless it is necessary, and then should be employed only to the extent needed. The *bin* he referred to has been translated by some scholars as "weapon" and by extension, "war". Laozi thought that war was not a good thing, and should be waged only when one must. One should put the approach of waging war under a bigger goal, and treat it with caution and deliberation. A quiet life lived without war or fighting is a good life.

Sun-Tzu believed that war would seriously undermine the power of both the winning and losing states, and there would be no guarantee that some people would not take advantage of his victory in the confusion of a war environment. Even the ablest rulers enjoying victory would find it difficult to overcome the after-effects of war, so, theoretically, war should not exist. However, the reality of the world is such that it does exist. That is why the Chinese sages advocated war being moderated and disciplined by benevolence and justice. This is China's unique philosophical contribution to the art of war.

Laozi said that as long as one assisted the emperor with justice and did not attempt to conquer the world with war, both political and state affairs could be easily resolved. One must remember that no good comes of war — crops are ruined and wild grass grows rampant in their place. After the passing of the army, fighting, killing and chaos continue in its wake.

Sun-Tzu (Sun Wu) wrote that the military leader who uses his forces skillfully will be able to ensure peace and the orderly maintenance of society. With this in mind, he should seize the opportunity to beat the enemy decisively. Just sages should help the emperor and his citizens reach a consensus whether to go to war or not; his citizens, being unafraid of the difficulties faced, would live or die to support that consensus.

Mencius says that benevolent gentlemen are matchless in the world, and sending forces further armed with benevolence to suppress armies not possessing this quality is an assurance of victory and can avoid the unnecessary loss of lives. His famous mottos, "benevolent gentlemen are matchless", and "a just cause enjoys great support, while an unjust one finds little", are familiar to almost every Chinese.

Traditional Chinese political culture always adheres to a people-centered policy. This policy asserts that "the people are the basis of the state", and "water can both carry a boat and sink it". That is why, in Chinese military culture, benevolence and justice are always used in an evaluation of a decision to go to war, in order to determine the probable benefit to the people. The ancient treatise on the art of war, Sima's *Art of War*, says that if one country attacks another while at the same time taking care to protect the citizens of the country under attack, then the attack is benevolent, and every means may be employed in the attack. Using war to stop war, though it is still conflict and death, can still find moral ground, and so such an attack is acceptable. It also says that while war may be waged when necessary, it still should not interrupt farming activities and aggravate the suffering of the people. This concern should of course apply to one's own citizens too.

Chinese military strategists always stress asking if the nature of a war is just and if the war is waged under the guidance of benevolence. That is why slogans like "punish the tyrants and comfort the people", "save the people from suffering", "release people from their pain", "punish only the responsible", and "do not harm the innocent", always appear during war. A just war may be waged while an unjust one may not. A just army attacks under a just cause — this has been the guiding thought of military strategists in all dynasties. This is the foundation for winning a war and keeping the morale of the people high.

The Chinese military philosophy first evaluates the moral standard of a war, and focuses on justice. However, Western military thought uses gain as their standard: this is the biggest difference between the two. Of course, this is not to say which standard is better; they are only reflections of different values. Chinese military culture uses benevolence and justice as guidance, and will not let war escalate out of control. The emphasis is not on its military strength, nor will it engage in uncontrolled violence — rather, it strives to win without fighting.

=

Strategic Thinking

in the Military Culture

Clausewitz maintained that war is the continuation of politics through another means. This statement has been universally accepted by statesmen and military strategists. When peaceful means are inadequate to solve the political issue, or if political strife has come to a point that the respective positions cannot be reconciled, then the parties will resort to war. War becomes the instrument for the solution of the political issue. Each party's aim in going to war is to settle the political issue in its favor. These were Clausewitz's views.

The first sentence of Sun-Tzu's *Art of War* is, "The art of war is of vital importance to the state. It is a matter of life and death, the road to either safety or to ruin. Hence it is a subject of inquiry which can on no account be neglected". It put war as a responsibility of the state and the nation as a whole, as a matter of great importance, necessary to the survival of the nation and must be considered carefully. This is the primary strategic thought in Chinese traditional military culture, which is much more cautious, comprehensive and profound than that of Clausewitz. No matter how acute and drastic the political conflict is, the life, future, and very existence of a nation must be carefully considered before resorting to arms. This concern not only exemplifies the peace-loving nature of the Chinese people, but also shows a deep understanding of the monster of war. Therefore, after comparing the strategic thoughts of both Clausewitz and Sun-Tzu, an English military theoretician said that of all the military strategists in the past, only Clausewitz could be a match for Sun-Tzu. However, the time of Clausewitz developing his theories and writing his book was a good 2,000 years after Sun-Tze's writings. Even so, some of his views lagged behind Sun-Tzu's, and some of them are already outdated. By comparison, Sun-Tzu presented a more intelligent and profound approach to the important issues of war — this fact endowed his writings with immortality.

Sun-Tzu's *Art of War* says, "the art of war is governed by five constant factors which must be taken into account in one's deliberations when seeking to determine the conditions faced in the field. These are: (1) The Moral Law; (2) Heaven; (3) Earth; (4) The Commander; (5) Method and Discipline." This is a treatise on developing a comprehensive strategy inclusive of considerations of politics, timing, geography, leaders and laws. There are in total 13 chapters in Sun-Tzu's *Art of War* that can be read today: Initial Estimations, Waging War, Planning Offensives, Military Disposition, Strategic Military Power, Vacuity and Substance, Military Combat, Nine Changes, Maneuvering the Army, Configurations of Terrain, Nine Terrains, Incendiary Attacks, and Employing Spies. It is clear that factors like politics, diplomacy and psychology had been made integral to the war — this makes it look much like the modern comprehensive overall war.

Under the influence of these thoughts, China produced generation after generation of good military strategists. In the Spring and Autumn Period, there was Sun Bin besides Sun Wu. Liu Bang, founder of the Western Han Dynasty praised the military strategist Zhang Liang as "planning strategies within a command tent, and ensuring victory on the battle front a thousand *li* away". Han Xin and Cao Cao were also famous military strategists. Zhuge Liang, in the Three Kingdoms, was depicted as wisdom incarnate. He comprehensively analysed wars from the standpoints of politics, economics, geography, culture, timing, geographic convenience and harmony in human relations, in order to promote the development of political thought and military theory in the future. This tradition has nurtured a great number of Chinese military strategists who understood strategy, politics and military affairs. They are referred to as "Confucian Generals", and their guidance to field military officers produced remarkable results in war. The so-called "Strategic Specialty and Military Expertise" is a good generalization describing this synergistic combination.

In the Chinese traditional military culture, apart from the importance of a comprehensive strategy, the function of tactics is also stressed: the "36 Tactics" are representative of those proven to be the most successful. These are plans to win by specific operational moves, to reach the goal of victory as much as possible without fighting, and to keep losses to a minimum.

Chinese military strategists always use benevolence as the moral standard underlying their strategies - winning and conquering other's army through strategy is benevolence. Winning through tactics is the highest state of war. While adhering to the guiding rule of "benevolence", the intelligence of the military strategist can be put to the best use. "All warfare is based on deception." So, tactics employed in the Chinese military culture are not simply examples of being cunning without principles and morals, but rather an approach to defend benevolence, loyalty and justice. So for over 2,000 years, military strategists had never argued about the morals of using military tactics. This is because military strategists have a consensus in using tactics. They maintain that using tactics is consistent with the ideal of benevolence, while paying attention only to fighting and killing without using tactics is not benevolent. Sun-Tzu said:

> The practice of raising a host of a hundred thousand men and marching them great distances entails heavy losses on the people and is a drain on the resources of the state. The daily expenditure will amount to a thousand ounces

of silver. There will be commotion at home and abroad, and men will drop down exhausted on the highways. As many as seven hundred thousand families will be impeded in their labor. Hostile armies may face each other for years, striving for the victory which is decided in a single day. This being so, to remain in ignorance of the enemy's condition simply because one grudges the outlay of a hundred ounces of silver in honors and emoluments, is the height of inhumanity. One who acts in this way is no leader of men, no help to his sovereign, and no master of victory.

This means malevolent to the utmost are those leaders who always raise 100,000 soldiers to wear down both the citizenry and the state's resources, hope to win the war by one battle and thereby gain personal fame and profit, while totally ignorant of the enemy's situation. They are not good generals, not qualified to assist the emperor. Even if they themselves are emperors, they are unlikely to enjoy victory.

We can see that Sun-Tzu focused attention on understanding the enemy's situation. One must be forearmed with knowledge of the conditions the enemy faces and his intentions. "Now this foreknowledge cannot be elicited from spirits; it cannot be obtained inductively from experience, nor by any deductive calculation. Knowledge of the enemy's disposition can be obtained only from other men." If one wants to have this prior knowledge, he must gain this intelligence from people who know the enemy's situation. Therefore, the spy becomes a necessity. The earliest treatise on espionage in the world appeared — in Sun-Tzu's *Art of War*, the Use of Spies.

"Knowing the enemy and yourself, one need not fear the result of a hundred battles", is a famous saying of Sun-Tzu. In order to know oneself, one must perceive everything about one's situation and condition; in order to know the enemy, one must employ military intelligence. This became an important adjunct to military operations. In both open and covert warfare, we should always bear in mind the basis of tactics — benevolence — which in turn is based on justice.

≡

The Influence of
China's Military Culture
on the World

　　Sun-Tzu's *Art of War* was very popular during the Warring States Period. It was introduced to Japan around the 7th century AD and was taught to the Japanese court. In order to rally his armies, the famous military strategist Takeda of the Japanese Warring States Period wrote on his flag the four characters for wind, forest, fire and mountain. These four characters are taken from Sun-Tzu's *Art of War*: "Let your speed be that of the wind, your unity that of the forest. In raiding and plundering, be like the fire; in immovability, a mountain". Japanese cartoons today frequently feature Sun-Tzu , and his writings are popular with both adults and children. After the 18th century, Sun-Tzu's *Art of War* was translated into French, English, German, Czech, and Russian, and was studied by military strategists all over the world. It is reported

A New Year's
picture: "Cao Cao's
army of one million
going down south
of the Yangtze
River"

that after reading this book, William II of Germany rued not having read the book earlier — he would not have lost in the First World War, he thought. On February 19, 1983, the Associated Press reported that the American military had altered its strategy, paying more attention to speed, mobility, and going behind the enemy's lines, and that its theoretical foundation was Sun-Tzu's *Art of War*.

A Western Sinologist serialized a book explicating the 36 Tactics. By the time he had reached the 18th tactic, his book was already attracting wide attention. Foreign statesmen were quoted as saying that this book would be very helpful to those in political circles. Chinese military culture once again surprised the world and its ancient intelligence shone again.

Japanese military scholars believe that, though Sun-Tzu's *Art of War* is old, it continues to be relevant to the modern world. People in Japanese economic circles sometimes plan their business tactics following the tactics described in Sun-Tzu's *Art of War*. Alert and perceptive leaders in other countries in the region, like Korea and Singapore, also actively apply Sun-Tzu's principles to issues related to their economies, and have experienced rewarding results.

Chapter Nine
Great Contributions to Mankind

Since the Chinese nation is one of the oldest still in existence, and the only one with an unbroken history through ancient and modern times, the experience, lessons and information it can provide to mankind must be abundant.

—

The Four Great Inventions of Ancient China

The whole world knows the four great inventions of ancient China — papermaking, printing, the compass and gunpowder.

Papermaking

It can be concluded from excavations that paper made of vegetable fiber appeared as early as the Western Han Dynasty. According to historical records, the man who first created paper from vegetable fiber was Cai Lun of the Eastern Han Dynasty. As a matter of fact, he may have modified and improved upon his forbears' experience in making paper with fiber, rather than being the actual inventor. Extensive use of paper for writing came after the Wei and Jin Dynasties. During the Tang Dynasty, China's papermaking technology made its way to the Arab world. After the Moors conquered Spain in the 11th century, they introduced the technology to Spain, set up papermaking operations there, and the technology gradually spread throughout all of Europe.

Paper produced in the Western Han Dynasty (206BC-25AD)

Printing

Printing was invented around the Sui and Tang Dynasties, and the technology used then was engraving printing. Around the middle of the eleventh century, Bi Sheng invented movable-type printing. During the Yuan Dynasty, printing was introduced to Korea, Japan and Europe.

A south-pointing
instrument —
the prototype of
the compass

The Compass

The "south-pointing fish" was invented in the early Song Dynasty, and a practical compass was developed soon after. It found a universal application in the seafaring industry. During the Northern Song Dynasty, many ships equipped with compasses plied trade routes through the South China Sea, the Indian Ocean and elsewhere. Arab traders embarked on Chinese ships to come to China to do business, and in China learned how to manufacture and utilize the compass. They then introduced it to their own lands and to Europe. The introduction of the compass has played an important role in the development of the world's maritime industry.

A firelock from the Yuan Dynasty

Gunpowder

Gunpowder was invented by a group of alchemists employed in making pills bestowing immortality. It was first produced before the Tang Dynasty, but the names of the inventors have not been recorded nor the exact year of invention. At around the eighth or ninth century AD, immortality pill-making technology was introduced to the Arab world, and the critical ingredient of gunpowder, niter, was introduced to the Arab world and Persia. However, only after the twelfth century do the historical records of Arab countries mention niter. They referred to it as "Chinese Snow"; the Persians called niter, "Chinese Salt". The method of making gunpowder was probably introduced there during the Southern Song Dynasty. The firearms of China and their manufacturing methods were introduced to the Arab world around the thirteenth century. The ancient Arab books on the art of war wrote that there were two kinds of firearms. One was the "Qidan Firelock", which was used in close confrontations; the other was the "Qidan Fire Arrow", which was used for longer distances. "Qidan" was the appellation that Arab and other nations gave China, and the so-called "Qidan Firelock" was precisely the same as the Chinese firelock. The invention of so-called "hot weaponry" should also be attributed to China. The Arabs introduced the methods of manufacturing gunpowder and firearms to the Europeans. This was several hundred years after the Chinese first started using gunpowder and firearms.

=

Other Inventions and Contributions in Chinese History

The inventions of the Chinese are not simply these four; there are many other contributions that China has made to the world. Whether in the physical sciences or social sciences, China has contributed its knowledge and discoveries to the benefit of mankind.

The civil system of government, which is now employed in countries all over the world, and is thought to be the most comprehensive system, was actually a development from ancient Chinese society. During the 2,000 years since the Qin and Han Dynasties, the political system of China has included central officials, the governance of regional provinces, the imperial civil examination system, a procedure for selecting and appointing officials according to established rules and regulations, a promotion system, the avoidance system, a framework regulating the compensation of officials, system of assessment and appraisal one for supervision system, and a variety of others. All these in total formed a complete, detailed, and comprehensive political system. The brilliant Chinese culture is underpinned by this very effective managerial system. Dr Sun Yat-Sen said a long time ago that "the current examination systems in different countries are almost all imitations of the British one, and the British examination system was learned from us Chinese." So, it is clear that the Chinese civil official system has been a great contribution to many countries.

The idea in Taoism of the two opposing and yet united poles of *yin* and *yang* has given enormous inspiration to the scientists of the world.

Confucianism provides mankind with the most complete political and philosophical system to understand oneself, personal relations and an ideal society. Confucius's "benevolence" and "manners", along with the idea of "loyalty" from Mencius all gave inspiration to mankind . No wonder that some Western scholars regard Confucius as the first milestone in the history of human thinking.

Apart from the four great inventions, porcelain is perhaps the invention most significant to the world. All primitive clans knew how to fire pottery made with clay, but the step from pottery to porcelain was a unique process invented by the Chinese. Over 3,000 years ago, China's ancestors had already learned to fire primitive porcelain from pottery making. Real porcelain did not appear until the late period of the Eastern Han Dynasty to the Wei and Jin Dynasties. From antiques excavated in the subterranean palace of the Famen Temple, Fufeng County, Xianyang, Shaanxi Province, we can see porcelain made some 1,200 years ago when the Tang Dynasty was in full flower. It is believed that the Persians started working with porcelain-making technology in the 11th century, while the Italians did not start to cover pottery clay with a kind of lead glaze until 1470, but that was not real porcelain. In 1712, French missionaries found out that porcelain could be made by using kaolin from the Kaolin Mountain, Jingdezhen, Jiangxi Province. They found ways to transport it to Europe and it was only then that the

Europeans manufactured real porcelain. As a result, the term "kaolin" was attached to the white clay universally used in the world's porcelain-making industry. That is why today's westerners call porcelain "china", which means that porcelain is China's unique invention, and that westerners have gained a better understanding of China through porcelain.

Silk was invented by China. As early as in the pre-historical legends, China's ancestors had learned to raise silkworms and to spin and weave silk. The legendary Lei Zu was the inventor of the technique of silkworm raising and silk spinning. Virgil, the famous poet of ancient Rome, imagined that silk was something flowing down from trees. When he wrote this, China was already using a silk-spinning machine and jacquard loom, had the technology for printing multiple colors, and was manufacturing silk products like brocades, yarn, satin and embroidery. In 1972, over 200 silk products were excavated in the Mawangdui Han tomb in Changsha. Among them there was an intact white silk yarn garment, which was as thin as cicada's wings and as soft and light as today's nylon scarf. The length of the garment was 128 centimeters, with a sleeve length of 190 centimeters, but its weight was only 49 grams. Also excavated were silk drawings with bright colors, and light and classical cup-shaped satins with diamond patterns. As early as 2,100 years ago, the country had mastered the sophisticated technique of silk weaving — aristocrats in the West were willing to pay gold of the same weight for the silks. The road used to transport silk connects the East and the West, the land and the sea, and is called the Silk Road. The ancient Greeks and Romans called China "seres", meaning "the country of silk". "Seres" is obviously the transliteration of the Chinese character *Si*. The English word "silk" in turn evolved from "seres". Silk connects China and the world. Today, China is still the largest producer of silk.

Tea was discovered in China. The names for tea in many languages today were borrowed from the Chinese dialects common to Guangdong and Southern Fujian. The history of China's ancestors' drinking tea goes back as far as some 4,000 years. In the Qin and Han Dynasties, China had already started growing the earliest tea bushes in the world and began producing tea. By the Tang Dynasty, the practice of drinking tea had become popular all over the country. Lu Yu wrote the first book specializing in tea — *The Classics of Tea*. In the 5th century AD, Chinese tea was introduced to Japan and Korea. Starting in the 17th century, tea was being sold to every region of America and Europe and the fashion of drinking tea had swept the whole world. Tea, coffee and cocoa are together called the Three Beverages. Admiring tea, tasting tea and discussing tea are all the embodiments of the unique philosophy of China's everyday normal life. A complete tea set unearthed in the subterranean palace of Famen Temple confirmed the usage of tea sets as early as the Tang Dynasty. There are five categories of Chinese tea: green tea, black tea, oolong tea, scented tea and brick tea. Every category can be further divided into several types, are processed in different ways, and are of different tastes. In other countries, only a few types of tea exist, such as black tea. So China is still a big country in tea and the tea culture.

Chinese medicine has also contributed greatly to the world. It is reported that open-skull surgery was performed in China as early as 3,000 years ago, and that anesthesia was widely used in the Eastern Han Dynasty. Recently, China also provided drugs like berberine and ephedrine to the world's medical circles in order to promote the welfare of mankind. Acupuncture and massage treatments from Chinese medicine are becoming more and more recognized by the world.

Perhaps the use of negotiable securities could be called China's fifth great invention. No matter whether the *fei qian* used in the Tang Dynasty, the *jiao zi, jiao ying, guan zi*, or *hui zi* used in the Song Dynasty, the *jiao chao* used in the Yuan Dynasty or the *bao chao* used in the Ming Dynasty, they were all more advanced than the negotiable securities (documents used to transfer value, as paper currency) used in other places in the world in the same period.

Advertisements and logos are also qualified to compete for the honor of being the fifth invention of China. The wind-facing and blowing *zhao zi* (flag with the shop's name on it hung at the doorstep of a shop) in the scroll of painting, "Life along the River during Qingming Festival", demonstrates that logos, advertisements and shop signs existed as early as the Song Dynasty. In drawings from the Song Dynasty, there are also clowns with the names of commercial products stuck on their backs as they swagger through the streets. Publishing houses also put advertisements in their books. There is an advertisement for spirits — "three bowls of spirits and one is drunk enough not to climb the hill" — in the novel *Heroes of the Marshes*. Shop signs were erected at the entrance of every wine shop, and advertisements promising to "provide comfortable accommodation for travelers and businessmen" always stood in front of inns. These were things that the rest of the world had not yet seen.

Soybeans and bean products also qualify to compete for the fifth great invention. This nutritious plant with low fat and high protein was first grown, processed and eaten by the Chinese, and was introduced to Europe through Japan. Today more than ever, soybean milk, bean sprouts and bean curd are popular in the world.

China had already manufactured distance-recording wagons and south-pointing wagons as early as 2,000 years ago. These are wooden machines that operate through the movement of an axis driven by the rotation of gears. It is said that Zhuge Liang (181-234, statesman and strategist during the period of the Three Kingdoms) also produced wooden oxen and gliding horses to carry army provisions. These devices could be called forefathers of the clutch, gear systems, and the odometer of modern vehicles.

As early as 4,000 to 5,000 years ago, China already had wooden ships. It is clear that the shipbuilding industry was already quite advanced by the Qin and Han Dynasties. Centers of shipbuilding activity then included some ten places like Chang'an, Suzhou, Fuzhou and Guangzhou. *History of Han: Records of Emperor Wudi* records that a ship named Yu Zhang was constructed, upon which a luxurious palace was built and 10,000 people could embark. The legend of the first emperor of the Qin Dynasty sending an expedition led by Xu Fu in search of paradise and the immortality pill could have been possible only after the capability to build large ships was attained. The story suggests the sophistication of Chinese shipbuilding at that time, and China's developed navigation skills. Ships in the Tang Dynasty began utilising paddlewheels. This was a huge innovation in shipbuilding technology. Paddlewheel ships appeared in Europe as late as the 15th or 16th centuries, 700 or 800 years later than in China. In the Song Dynasty, watertight compartments in sailing ships appeared: and these appeared in the West only in the 18th century. Ocean-going ships in the Song Dynasty used the compass for navigation: this was two centuries earlier than the West adopted this innovation. During the Tang, Song, Yuan, Ming and Qing Dynasties, China floated the largest fleets in the world. From the 7th century on, Chinese fleets frequently appeared in the ocean. Foreign merchants also used Chinese ships for transport and travel between points in Southeast Asia and the Indian Ocean.

Bridge-building technology in ancient China also led the world. Chinese bridges cover the whole country. The Zhaozhou Bridge in Hebei Province, the Guangji Bridge in Guangdong Province, and the Luoyang Bridge and Anping Bridge in Fujian Province may all been seen as the first models of bridge-building.

The Zhaozhou Bridge in Hebei Province was constructed by the artisan Li Chun of the Sui Dynasty, and has already weathered some 1,300 years of trials and hardships. The length of this single-span stone bridge is 50.82 meters, and the span is 37.02 meters. The whole bridge presents a beautiful and magnificent appearance. Its size alone is worthy of the world's admiration, and the design of two small arches sitting on each of the shoulders of the single large arch is even more ingenious. This design technique is highly praised even by modern experts in bridge-building.

The Guangji Bridge of the Han River, east of Chaozhou, Guangdong Province was built in the Song Dynasty. With a length of 518 meters, it is a combination of a fixed segment and floats — a portion of the bridge is a pontoon composed of 18 boats. When boats in the river pass, the pontoon moves and gives way to the boats; after the passing of the boats, the pontoon closes. This design made the passage of river traffic, as well as pedestrians and land vehicles, a reality. This ingenious combination of a solid bridge with a floating, moveable section, was the world's first.

The Luoyang Bridge was built in the Northern Song Dynasty some 900 years ago. It is situated at the estuary of the Luoyang River in Quanzhou, Fujian Province and is a masterpiece of beam bridges. The bridge support was built upon a 500 meter-long underwater embankment.

China also built cable bridges made of different materials (like bamboo, cane, and iron). The cable bridge, together with the arch bridge and beam bridge, is one of the three basic architectural styles of bridges. From ancient times to now, bridges belonging to these three categories span the waterways and valleys of the country.

Pi is the ratio of the circumference of a circle to its diameter. The level of accuracy in the measurement of *pi* is an indicator of the level of mathematical development in different ages. Liu Hui in the Wei and Jin Dynasties proposed the "Circle-Cutting Method", which got the circumference by calculating the ratio of the length of the sides of a regular polygon to the diameter of the circle. Then from the inner-circle regular hexahedron, Liu doubled the number of sides of the regular polygon repeatedly: 12 sides, 24 sides, 48 sides, 96 sides — the more the sides, the closer the circumference of the regular polygon was to the circumference of the circle. When he reached 192nd sides around the inner circle, he had shown the value of *pi* to be 3.14124. He later did a calculation with 3,072 sides, and reached a more accurate value of *pi* — 3.14159.

The person who contributed most to the calculation of *pi* was Zu Chongzhi (429-500). During the Southern and Northern Dynasties, populations were migrating southward, and the Chinese economic and cultural center was gradually shifting to the Yangtze River valley. Zu Chongzhi spent his whole life in the Southern Dynasty and made great accomplishments in science. He proceeded from the value of *pi* calculated by Liu Hui and put forward two

values of *pi*: one was the approximate ratio 22/7, which had already been calculated by someone before him, and the other was the more precise ratio 355/113, which was Zu's unique accomplishment and the most accurate until the 16th century. He went even further in calculating the approximate value of *pi*, and denoted it by the mathematical sign, i.e. 3.1415926< *pi* <3.1415927. William Oughtred of Germany and Adriaen Anthonisz of the Netherlands reached this conclusion at the end of the 16th century, 1,000 years after Zu's death. That is why the value of 355/113 was called by the famous Japanese mathematician Mikami Yoshio as the "Zu's Ratio", which was recognized by the whole world.

The Xia Dynasty used ten days as one *xun* - this calendar system has lasted in China until now. The inscriptions on tortoise shells and ancient bronze objects in the Shang Dynasty initially used 13 single characters and their combinations to record any natural number within 100,000 (i.e. 一 [1], 二 [2], 三 [3], 四 [4], 五 [5], 六 [6], 七 [7], 八 [8], 九 [9], 十 [10], 百 [100], 千 [1,000] and 万 [10,000]). This signaled the birth of the decimal system. After the Qin and Han Dynasties, China established a comparatively complete decimal system. Using the decimal system, China made its own calculator — the abacus.

The chemical techniques used in making the "immortality-pill", the invention of the first seismograph, the science of genetics and breeding, the earliest recording of astronomical phenomena, the lunar calendar of China (include the Great Ming Calendar by Zu Chongzhi) — all played an important and profound role in the world's history.

There were many other inventions, such as lacquer, playing cards, chopsticks, kites, leather-silhouette show, wallpaper, the folding umbrella, paper fan, sedan chair and soccer. All these ancient inventions have been recorded by Dr. Joseph Needham of Great Britain in his monumental work *Science and Civilization in China*. This respected scholar said, "It can be proved with little effort that these inventions of China had long surpassed those of Europe in the same age, and this holds especially true before the 15th century".

An American scholar has also said with emotion that how lean and shabby Western civilization would be if westerners had not had these things. Some of these things provided them endless pleasure, some of them were rich in the value of both their use and artistic enjoyment, and some others had completely changed their way of life, and became the foundation of modern civilization.

China has contributed much to the world, and it has also learned a great deal from other countries.

≡

Scientific Thought

in Ancient China and

Its Influences

The idea unifying two integral parts, man and nature, was the systematic view of the world in the traditional culture of China. Such thought allowed China to develop a set of systems that are different from western science and culture. Its characteristics lie in the ability to think systematically, comprehensively and dialectically and take an integrated view of the world.

Chinese medicine is representative of the scientific thinking system of China. According to Chinese medicine, the human body is a unification of the harmony of the two poles of *yin* and *yang*. Health means the balance and harmony of *yin* and *yang*. The upset of this balance, or more *yin*, less *yang*, or vice versa is what creates ill health. The human body is a small system compared to the large system of the universe, but Chinese medicine discovered the connections between

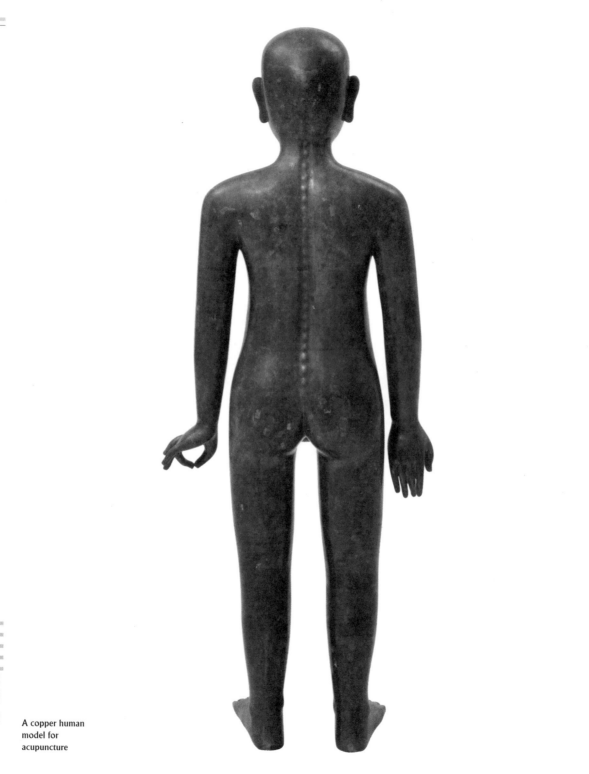

A copper human
model for
acupuncture

different parts of the human body through main and collateral channels and acupuncture points. It also discovered the dialectical connections between *yin*, *yang*, and the Five Elements, and the theory of what each produces and how it is overcome by the others. The East, West, South, North, Middle; Dawn, Dusk, Noon, Afternoon, Evening; Metal, Wood, Water, Fire, Earth; and me, soh, doh, ray, la are all connected to symptoms of disease and the fluctuations of the emotions of the human body. They are also related to the tastes of medicine (sour, hot, bitter, sweet and salt). Different parts of the human body are also connected with the skin, hair and organs. For instance, the liver is connected with the eyes, the heart with the tongue, the lungs with the large intestines, and the stomach with the skin and hair. So, the way of treating diseases in Chinese medicine is not treating the head when the head hurts, or the feet when the feet ache. Instead, in order to get a comprehensive idea it uses four methods of diagnosis: "observation of the patient's complexion, expression, movements, tongue, etc.; auscultation and olfaction; interrogation; and pulse-feeling and palpation". In addition to feeling the patient's pulse, looking at his/her complexion, smelling his/her body odor, asking the history of diseases, the symptoms, diet and daily life, and the fluctuation of his moods, the doctor has to consider as well his age, habits, where he lives and the season, in order to determine the cause of the disease. When filling out a prescription, the doctor will also consider the location, the time of giving drugs, the seasons, the constitution of the patient, and the main and auxiliary roles among the drugs. When one has a cough from tracheitis, Chinese medicine will always use medication to moisten the intestines and induce catharsis, in order to relieve the temper in the lungs; and licorice root, among all the drugs, would be invariably used. When one gets red and swollen eyes, drugs to appease the liver will be used. This way of dialectical treatment and full-body adjustment illustrates the principle of harmony between man and nature in Chinese culture. The theory of acupuncture and the theory of main and collateral channels (regarded as a

Great
Contributions
to Mankind

233

network of passages through which one's vital energy flows and along which acupunctural points are distributed) are the products of this system of thinking. Chinese medicine ensures that the life of the Chinese nation will last forever and prosper. Its unique achievements are being paid more and more attention in many different countries. There are factions like Tibetan, Mongolian and Korean medicine, all converging to form a unified and comprehensive system of Chinese medicine. This unified system will become one of the great treasures in the history of medicine. A policy of combining traditional with Western medicine has been implemented. This move has brought about cooperation with Western medicine and modern science, setting traditional Chinese medicine on a more correct and scientific road.

The ideas of comprehensive thinking, universal connections and mutual restraining and complementing in Chinese culture are being given more and more attention by scholars all over the world. The advancement of science is making a number of frontier or interdisciplinary disciplines become new scientific

234

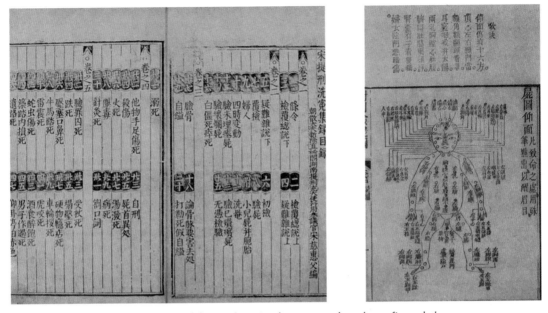

categories. The rise of chaos and fuzzy theories have tested and confirmed the correctness of ancient Chinese thoughts. The Supreme Ultimate diagram composed of integrated and connected *yin* and *yang* fish perfectly embodied the antithesis, complement, and endless development of the world in the two poles. In 1937, the founder of modern quantum theory and quantum mechanics, the Danish physicist Niels Bohr, visited China and was greatly surprised and impressed by the Chinese theory of two poles. He thought that the issues dealt with by Laozi of Taoism had already anticipated the atomic theory in the issue of methodology. He realized that the ancient intelligence of Chinese people and Western modern science involved very profound correlations. He chose the Supreme Ultimate pattern of China as his family emblem, and kept his admiration for Chinese traditional culture all his life.

The leading position occupied by Chinese science slipped behind after reaching the modern age, and the causes are various. The lack of metaphysical thinking is one. The way of thinking with more generalization and less specific analysis and an underdeveloped taxonomy inhibited the development of natural science.

Now the new century is probably time for China to catch up again. The combination of Oriental and Western thinking should help China's natural science and technology develop more rapidly.

A Magnificent Future

Chapter Ten

In the history of the development of human civilization, there have existed four great ancient civilizations: the Egyptian, Babylonian, Indian, and Chinese civilizations.

The ancient Egyptian civilization disintegrated as early as the 6th century BC. Its history lasted for about 3,500 years, and now only the pyramids stand under the moonlight: their secrets still hide in the haze of history. The ancient Babylonian civilization was overthrown by the Hittites in approximately 1595 BC, and the reign of the Hittites was in turn overthrown by invaders from the sea. The once-brilliant ancient Babylonian civilization disappeared. The Gupta Dynasty of ancient India once glowed brilliantly in the east, but was overthrown at the beginning of the 6th century AD and was split and scattered into many small kingdoms. The glow of the ancient Indian civilization dimmed.

After all the disasters it encountered, only the Chinese nation survived. It weathered countless storms and hardships, but has always been able to survive reverses to its development, and after 5,000 years, it still looks young.

The reason that the Chinese civilization has such strong staying power lies in its ability to absorb and assimilate others. The main body of the Chinese civilization, the Han culture, was formed by integrating and merging with many other Chinese cultures. The process is ongoing and will last forever. In the Xia, Shang and Zhou Dynasties, the Hua Xia nation had already fused the tribes of the so-called "Man, Yi, Rong, Di", but preserved the characteristics of each of these nations and so formed a unified Chinese society.

In the Spring and Autumn and the Warring States Periods, the powers in the Central Plains, the Yi ethnic groups in the east, the Rong in the west, the Man in the south and the Di in the north constantly waged wars against one another and yet later fused with one another. After some 500 years of shakeup and consolidation, the unprecedented unification and power of the Qin and Han Dynasties was finally formed. The Han Dynasty incessantly fought the Huns, and

Left: The Great Wall

the south-migrating Huns were gradually absorbed into the Chinese nation. The policy of respecting Confucianism only affected the development of the Chinese civilization, whose core is Confucianism. Adherence to Confucianism set the stage for prosperous development.

From the Qin and Han Dynasties to the Wei and Jin Dynasties, the development of culture came to a trough. After this came the phase of the five northern tribes throwing the Chinese nation into disorder. Another bout of shakeup and consolidation occurred in the Southern and Northern Dynasties. This period was one of unprecedented, active cultural fusion within the Chinese nation. Northerners integrated into the Han nation and vice versa; the Persian culture in the west, the cultures of the western regions, and the cultures of Xianbei, Qiang and Di in the north, and Miao and Li in the south, converged in the Central Plains. The consolidation of all these groups formed the glorious culture of the Tang Dynasty. The opening up of the Tang Dynasty reached the apogee in Chinese history. Buddhism, Christianity and Islam spread across China, and the discourses of three doctrines of Confucianism, Buddhism and Taoism generated a philosophical debate. The Chang'an of that time was really the capital of the world, and had become the showcase of different world cultures. Of the million people living in Chang'an at that time, 20,000 to 50,000 were foreigners or immigrants, which is some number even today.

From the Sui and Tang Dynasties to the Five Dynasties, the development of culture started to wane again. The theory of Neo-Confucianism was formed and consolidated by Cheng Hao, Cheng Yi and Zhu Xi in the Song Dynasty. With Confucianism at its core, Neo-Confucianism also included Buddhism and Taoism. The Mongolian culture of the Yuan Dynasty used the system of following the Han practice in ceremony and law, contributing to the Chinese civilization, whose core was the Han culture. In the Ming Dynasty, society was still centered on Neo-Confucianism, but because of the rigidity of this school, it dissolved from maturity to corruption. It was no longer able to accommodate the rapid development of the urban economy under burgeoning commercial activity. Conversely, the citizen culture with strong democratic and mercantile sense became especially active. This was embodied in novels and dramas of the Ming Dynasty. The realistic exposure and criticism of Neo-Confucianism, the advocacy of the beauty of humanity, the realistic depiction of the mercantile economy, emerging merchant class, craftsmen, and the glorification of love — all showed that the Chinese civilization in the late period of the Ming Dynasty was facing a new phase of absorbing and assimilating new ideas. The development of Chinese science and technology also entered a new phase. Scientists like Xu Guangqi, Song Yingxing, the geologist Xu Xiake, and the medical expert Li Shizhen all appeared in that era. The times called for an outstanding thinker to formulate a theory that was geared to the needs of the age and could provide guidance for the future. The new theory should replace Neo-Confucianism and stimulate the advent of capitalism. Such a person did appear who could have become that type of thinker — he was Li Zhi (1527-1602). He sharply criticized the practice of Neo-Confucianism and directly aimed his criticism at Confucius. He strongly criticized the "big" Confucian scholars from Han Yu through the Song and Ming Dynasties, and the Confucian orthodoxy advocated by Zhu Xi. He proposed the egalitarianism of human society, i.e. "every man is a ready sage", and "every man is equipped with wise thought". He advocated equality between men and women, and opposed the tradition of unduly stressing agriculture and ignoring commerce. His pointed criticism could be regarded as the strongest since the publication of *Asking Confucius* written by Wang Chong in the Eastern Han Dynasty. This is why Li was persecuted and later he died in prison. His thinking was perceptive, but, like other Chinese philosophers, he was also entangled in a strange, vicious circle of only repeating or criticizing the thoughts and writings of others without having original ideas. Therefore, he was

A photocopy of *A Dream of Red Mansions* collated by Cheng Jia

unable to formulate a comprehensive theory of his own and was not an original thinker. He was not like the enlightening Western scholars who became vanguards in opposing feudalism and advocating capitalism. Li Zhi didn't go further to become a Chinese thinker with a democratic sense, still less were there a group of independent thinkers in China at that time. Consequently there was no intellectual shakeup like the Western Enlightenment. Though the trend in other countries had shown the way for the development of citizens' culture in China, the rigid and powerful influence of feudal rulers and their theoretical system of Neo-Confucianism (Idealist Philosophy) suppressed the development of any advances in thinking.

In order to stabilize and strengthen their regimes, rulers in the Qing Dynasty used a policy of alternating coercion and mollification. In the process of consolidating their power, these emperors attempted to preserve the social habits, the traditional culture and moral dictates of the Han people in order to avoid conflict among various nationalities. So, during some 200 years of the reign of the Qing Dynasty, great academic and cultural achievements were made. The Plain Learning (or textual criticism or research of the classical school) of the Qing Dynasty and the Idealist Philosophy of Song and Ming Dynasties shone upon each other. The theories of pragmatism and opposing pretentious discourse proposed by scholars Huang Zongxi, Gu Yanwu and Wang Fuzhi changed the style of scholarship. Novels like *A Dream of Red Mansions* and *The Scholars* shone with extraordinary splendor, and legendary works like *Peach Blossom Fan* and *Chang Sheng Dian* showed outstanding achievements in the circle of drama. Novels of censure, which became popular in the late period of the Qing Dynasty, such as *Revealing the*

Original Shape in Officialdom, and, *The Travels of Lao Chan,* contributed by satirizing officialdom, especially the corrupt behavior of officials, and were the impetus for political reform. The school of studying Confucian classics in modern script advocated by Gong Zizhen, Wei Yuan and Kang Youwei presented even better the new face of intellectuals on the eve of the great social revolution. In general, the Qing Dynasty presided over the fusion of the Man culture and the Han culture, but the Chinese nation's culture grew slowly. The cultural wane was worsened by the rulers' closing up policy that restricted communication with foreign cultures.

Apart from constantly integrating the cultures of different ethnic groups of China, the country also incessantly absorbed the meritorious aspects of foreign cultures, and made them part of the local, Chinese culture. The Chinese civilization is one that always learns from other civilizations.

There are three major religions in the world: Christianity, Islam and Buddhism. It could be said that these religions are the three pillars of the world's religious culture. These three religions, in spreading outside their places of origin, have all encountered bloody wars in every part of the world. However, these three religions entered China with peace, and no religious war has taken place during the long history of China. Buddhism was introduced to China even on its own initiative. This is an unusual occurrence in the world's history, and should be food for thought.

Islam was introduced to China approximately in the middle of the 7th century. During the Wu De years of the Tang Dynasty (618-626), Mohammed sent Four Sages to China: the first sage did missionary work in Guangzhou, the second in Yangzhou, and the third and the fourth in Quanzhou. When the maternal uncle of Mohammed escorted the Koran to China under order, he was received warmly by Emperor Tang Taizhong and was permitted to set up mosques in places like Chang'an, Jiangning and Guangzhou. Today, Guangzhou still has the earliest relic of the Islam — the Huaisheng Mosque (or Guangta Mosque). Its height is about 55 meters. Standing prominently among many tall buildings, it tells people of the world of the broad mind of the Chinese during the flowering of the Tang Dynasty.

Christianity was introduced to China at almost the same time. In the Forest of Steles in Xi'an, there is one stele called "Nestorianism of Da Qin Gains Popularity in China". The inscription on it gives an account of how the Nestorian clergyman Abraham was welcomed by Emperor Tang Taizhong and a temple was ordered to be built. On one side of this stele was the name of the clergyman, which was carved in the Syrian language. As a matter of fact, Abraham was not the first Christian to do missionary work in China. As early as the beginning of the 5th century, Nestorianism had already spread into Luoyang from the western regions. Later, the Roman Pope Nicolas IV sent Giovanni da Montecorvino of the Franciscan order to China in the Yuan Dynasty. He was appointed bishop of the Chinese diocese and set up parishes in Dadu, Quanzhou and Hangzhou. This Italian died of illness in Beijing 40 years later. Odorico da Pordenone , successor to Giovanni da Montecorvino, was one of the four famous European travelers in the Middle Ages and was as famous as Marco Polo. He arrived at Dadu in 1325 and wrote a book *Journeys to the East*, which highly praised the richness and prosperity of China. This is a book to compete with *Marco Polo Travels*. After Odorico, there were Matthew Ricci of the Ming Dynasty and Johann Adam Schall von Bell, who lived during the transition from the Ming Dynasty to Qing Dynasty. Both were clergymen of great renown, and their tombs are still well-preserved in Beijing.

The story of Xuan Zhang going on a pilgrimage to India to bring back Buddhist scriptures is known in every household of China. It shows the pious respect that China accorded Buddhism, which originated in India. Xuan Zhang's original name was Chen Wei. He became a monk at the age of thirteen. As he gradually grew dissatisfied with dissensions between various Buddhist sects in China, he decided to go to India to get the real Buddhist scriptures. He left Chang'an at the age of 25, and after numerous difficulties and obstacles, finally arrived in India. He studied in India for 15 years, traveling to some 70 kingdoms in India and became a famous enlightened monk. He left India to return to China in 643 AD, and arrived at Chang'an in the first month of the year 645. Under the order of Emperor Tang Taizhong, he wrote *Records on the Western Regions*, in which he recorded his visits to 110 cities, regions and countries, and wrote of 28 others based on second-hand reports. He presided over the translation of 75 Buddhist scriptures and built the Da Yan Pagoda as a repository for these scriptures. He also translated the works of Laozi of China, and the long-lost Buddhist scripture, *The Awakening of Faith* into Sanskrit and introduced them to India.

Buddhism experienced ebbs and flows in China. After reform by Huineng, the 6th grandmaster of the Chan sect of Buddhism, the process of localization was finally complete. Buddhism became a genuine part of Chinese culture with Chinese characteristics, and joined Confucianism and Taoism in becoming one of the three mainstream schools of thought in China.

Islam also tried to align itself with Chinese customs, and it was ultimately accepted. After it had established a foothold in China, a new ethnic group using the Han language but worshiping Islam arose in China — the Huis.

Other religions, such as Zoroastrianism and Manichaeanism, which are popular in the western regions, also peacefully entered China, and the Chinese civilization with a mind as broad as the sea also accepted them.

Every nation will experience a convoluted process of understanding in dealing with foreign cultures. The way that Catholicism in the Middle Age treated dissenting thinking was most barbaric. The large-scale religious massacres of the Middle Age were directed at reformists in the Catholic Church, or the advocates of other religious ideas. The precursor of modern astronomy, Giordano Bruno, was burned alive by a religious magistrate's court, but Matthew Ricci's missionary work in China was respected by the Chinese people in the Ming Dynasty. Under the auspices of royalty, he advocated theories of astronomy that debated the traditional calendric system and were finally vindicated by facts. After Matthew Ricci, there came Johann Adam Schall von Bell. With the support of Emperor Shun Zhi of the Qing Dynasty, he debated officials on the Terrace for Astronomical Observation and proved his claims on astronomical phenomena with facts. After his death, another priest — Ferdinand Erbiest — carried on his efforts by supervising the construction of many astronomical instruments. Today, they still stand at the ancient observatory in Beijing, and have become symbols of the scientific and astronomical achievements of the Chinese nation. The attitude with which the Chinese in the late Ming Dynasty and early Qing Dynasty treated dissenting thoughts stood in stark contrast with the occurrences of the dark Middle Ages of Europe. It is clear that the Chinese civilization is an enlightened one that accepts and absorbs meritorious thoughts from many other civilizations.

The whole secret of the endless prosperity of the Chinese nation lies first in the rationality of the mainstream traditional Chinese culture, second in its adeptness in fusing disparate Chinese subcultures into one, and third in its ability to accept, absorb and reform foreign cultures.

The development of Chinese society by the process of absorbing the valuable merits of other civilizations has given the country its strong vitality, so the country's resurrection was inevitable. Tradition is not a past, but a movement, a continued existence, a process which connects the history of the past, today and the future. The development of Chinese civilization is never broken, nor is the process by leaps and bounds, but a process of inheritance and gradual development. It does not abandon the outstanding creations of mankind, but constantly absorbs new elements in order to perfect itself. This should be the rule for the development of mankind.

Today, the sun in Asia is breaking through the clouds and rising once again. Hundreds of years of disasters were a trial. China's ancestors used to enjoin the people with passion that "the heaven is full of vigor, thus gentlemen should strive unceasingly to become stronger."

Now what China needs is not to abandon its past or its culture, nor to indiscriminately accept the ideas of the West. It should, in the process of facing the impact of different civilizations, examine itself, abandon things no longer useful, and while maintaining its advantage, adopt the useful aspects presented by foreign cultures, in order to create a new Chinese civilization.